FUNDAMENTALS OF LINGUISTICS

Raj Kumar Sharma

ATLANTIC
PUBLISHERS & DISTRIBUTORS (P) LTD

ATLANTIC
PUBLISHERS & DISTRIBUTORS (P) LTD
7/22, Ansari Road, Darya Ganj, New Delhi
Tel.: +91-11-4077 5252, 2327 3880
E-mail: orders@atlanticbooks.com
Web: www.atlanticbooks.com

Reprint 2025

Published by Atlantic Publishers & Distributors (P) Ltd.

Printed & bound in India by Atlantic Print Services

Dedicated to

the sweet memories of the days
I spent under the impervious umbrella of
my grandmother (Nani) Chandrapati Devi
whose love I treasure most.

Preface

This book has been designed to introduce the concepts of linguistics in a simple language and lucid style. Linguistics as a discipline claims to make a scientific study of language, and so, the book presents different aspects of language in a matter-of-fact way, i.e. in a highly objective manner. Over the years, linguistics has brought forth many new terms which are quite specific to this subject, and a clear concept of these terms becomes a precondition for the learners to develop an insight into the contents of this discipline. Such linguistic terms have been presented in a descriptive and analytical manner with sufficient examples. At many places, charts and figures have been given as supplements to clarify the subtle concepts. The simplest possible vocabulary has been used throughout the book, so that the learners may not have to struggle to understand the meaning. All of these efforts have been made with the objective of familiarizing the learners with the basic elements of linguistics.

The subject matter has been divided into eleven chapters which are scientifically sequenced and well-organized. The latest possible information related to the topics dealt with has been incorporated with elucidation. Further, it is relevant to mention that linguistics is comparatively an emerging branch of knowledge in which much research is underway, and so, there is a considerable difference of opinion among the linguists over several concepts, theories and their ways of analysis. However, an attempt has been made here to avoid controversy by presenting the topics in the most convincing and acceptable manner.

The book will be useful to the university students of all the levels (undergraduate and postgraduate) as not only does it introduce the fundamental concepts, but also talks about them in considerable details.

Finally, in spite of all the precautions taken in writing this book in order to make it flawless, it would be unwise to claim that it is immune to criticism. Therefore, the suggestions of readers and critics intended to improve the quality of the book will be highly appreciated.

I am thankful to Dr. K.R. Gupta, Honorary Adviser, Atlantic Publishers and Distributors (P) Ltd., and Mr. Harjeet Singh, Publication Co-ordinator, for publishing the book in a short time.

Raj Kumar Sharma

Acknowledgements

The realization of ideas in the form of a book is not an easy task as it requires much physical and mental exercise. By and large, it becomes a team work, and so, I cannot be oblivious of the contributions made by many of my well-wishers whose constant encouragement and support proved to be an inexhaustible source of inspiration and energy for me. In this regard, I sincerely recognize the efforts of Dr. Bhagwan Prasad Majumdar, Dr. Afroz Ashrafi, Dr. Bhushan Singh, Dr. Samir Kr. Sharma, Dr. Asra Mouda, Shri Jai Gopal Rai and Mr. Ramniwas Singh. Further, I appreciate the contribution of Prof. Syed Sahab Haider and Dr. Shailendra Kr. Mukul, who went through the whole manuscript and came out with valuable suggestions. I owe a deep sense of gratitude to the Faculties of erstwhile CIEFL, Hyderabad, whose enlightening lectures helped me develop an insight into the nuances of linguistics.

I am also thankful to my parents whose blessings keep on fertilizing my imaginative faculty. My acknowledgements will remain incomplete if I do not express my indebtness to Bibha, Pratyush and Shreya who thoroughly missed me during my preoccupation with this project. My thanks are equally due to my dear colleagues and affectionate students with whom I interact constantly, which substantially adds to my professional maturity, reflected in this book.

Raj Kumar Sharma

Contents

Preface *v*

Acknowledgements *vii*

1. All about Language **1**

1.1 What is Language? 1

1.2 Characteristics of Language 4

1.3 The Language of Animals 7

1.4 Difference between Language and a Language 9

1.5 The Functions of Language 9

Exercises 10

2. The World of Linguistics **12**

2.1 What is Linguistics? 12

2.2 The Scientific Nature of Linguistics 13

2.3 Scope of Linguistics 15

2.4 Levels of Linguistic Analysis 17

2.5 Major Branches of Linguistics 19

2.5.1 Sociolinguistics 20

2.5.2 Psycholinguistics 22

2.5.3 Stylistics 23

2.5.4 Applied Linguistics 24

2.6 The Relevance of Studying Linguistics 25

Exercises 28

3. A Brief History of Linguistics 29

3.1 The Approach of Classical Schools of Thought 29

3.2 Linguistics through the Middle Ages and Renaissance 31

3.3 Emergence of Linguistics as a Science in the 19th Century 32

3.4 Structuralism of the First-half of the 20th Century 33

3.5 Cognitivism of the Second-half of the 20th Century 34

Exercises 35

4. Major Concepts in Linguistics 37

4.1 Synchrony and Diachrony 37

4.2 Langue and Parole 39

4.3 Competence and Performance 40

4.4 Syntagmatic and Paradigmatic Relationship 41

4.5 Substance and Form 42

4.6 Linguistic Sign and Symbol 43

4.7 Signifier and Signified 44

Exercises 45

5. Phonetics 46

5.1 What is Phonetics? 46

5.2 Speech Production Mechanism 47

5.3 The Organs of Speech 48

5.4 Description of Speech Sounds 51

5.4.1 Description of Consonant Sounds 52

5.4.2 Description of Vowel Sounds 55

5.5 The Concept of Cardinal Vowels 58

5.6 The Concept of Diphthongs 59

5.7 The Concept of Triphthongs 59

5.8 Phonetic Transcription 60

Exercises 61

6. Phonology of English 63

6.1 Phonetics and Phonology 63

6.2 Description of English Sounds 64

6.2.1 English Consonants 64

6.2.2 English Vowels 68

6.3 Some Fundamental Concepts in Phonology 74

6.3.1 Phoneme 75

6.3.2 Allophone 75

6.3.3 Minimal Pair 76

6.3.4 Phonotactics 76

6.3.5 Phonetic Environment 76

6.3.6 Syllable 77

6.3.7 Aspiration 77

6.4 Phonemic Analysis 77

6.4.1 The Principle of Contrastive Distribution 78

6.4.2 The Principle of Complementary Distribution 78

6.4.3 The Principle of Free Variation 79

6.5 Phonemic Transcription 79

6.6 Prosodic or Supra-segmental Features 80

6.6.1 Stress 80

6.6.2 Rhythm 81

6.6.3 Intonation 82

6.7 Some Distinct Features of Connected Speech 84

6.7.1 Assimilation 84

6.7.2 Elision 85

6.7.3 Juncture 86

Exercises 86

7. **Morphology** 89
7.1 What is Morphology? 89
7.2 Some Important Concepts of Morphology 89
7.2.1 Morpheme 89
7.2.2 Morph 90
7.2.3 Allomorphs 91
7.2.4 Lexeme 91
7.2.5 Affixation 92
7.3 Classification of Morphemes of English Language 93
7.3.1 Free and Bound Morphemes 93
7.3.2 Lexical and Functional Morphemes 94
7.3.3 Derivational and Inflectional Morphemes 94
7.3.4 Class Changing and Class Maintaining Morphemes 96
7.3.5 Some Important Prefixes and Suffixes in English 97
7.3.5.1 Prefixes Frequently Used 97
7.3.5.2 Suffixes Frequently Used 99
7.4 Identification of Morphemes 101
7.4.1 The Concepts of Root, Stem and Base 102
7.4.2 Tree-diagrams of Morphemes 102
7.5 Morphophonemics 105
7.6 Formation of Words in English Language 108
Exercises 111

8. **Syntax** 114
8.1 What is Syntax? 114
8.2 The Constituents of a Sentence 114
8.2.1 Phrasal Constituents 114
8.2.2 Clausal Constituents of Sentences 123
8.3 Some Theories of Syntactic Analysis 125
8.3.1 Immediate Constituent (IC) Analysis 126

8.3.2 Phrase Structure Rule 127
8.3.3 Transformational Generative Grammar 131
8.3.3.1 The Concept of Transformational Generative 132
8.3.3.2 Transformational Rules 133
Exercises 139

9. Chomsky's Universal Grammar 142

9.1 What is Universal Grammar (UG)? 142
9.2 The Basis of UG Theory 143
9.3 The Notion of Principles and Parametres 145
9.3.1 Structure Dependency 145
9.3.2 Headedness Principle 146
9.3.3 Embedding Principle 146
9.3.4 Projection Principle 146
9.3.5 Locality Principle 147
9.3.6 Head Parameter 147
9.3.7 Pro-drop Parameter 148
9.4 UG and Language Acquisition 149
9.5 Some Major Theories of UG 151
9.5.1 X-bar Theory 151
9.5.2 Theta (θ) Theory 155
9.5.3 Government and Case Theory 157
9.5.4 Binding Theory 159
9.6 Minimalism: The Latest Innovation 161
Exercises 163

10. Semantics 164

10.1 What is Semantics? 164
10.2 The Meaning of Meaning 165
10.3 Some Concepts of Semantics 166
10.3.1 Semantics and Pragmatics 167
10.3.2 Sentence, Utterance and Proposition 168

10.3.3 Text and Discourse 169
10.3.4 Reference and Sense 170
10.3.5 Denotation and Connotation 171
10.3.6 Entailment and Presupposition 172
10.4 Semantic Classification of Words 172
10.5 Semantic Theories 176
10.5.1 Referential Theory 176
10.5.2 Componential Analysis Theory 177
10.5.3 Contextual Theory 178
10.5.4 Transformational Generative Theory 179
Exercises 181

11. Writing System (Graphology) 183

11.1 The Significance of Writing System 183
11.2 A Brief History of Writing 184
11.2.1 Ancient Writing System 185
11.2.2 Modern Writings 187
11.2.2.1 Morphemic Writing 187
11.2.2.2 Syllabic Writing 188
11.2.2.3 Alphabetic Writing 188
11.3 Some Concepts in Writing System 190
11.3.1 Grapheme 190
11.3.2 Allograph 190
11.3.3 Digraph 190
11.4 English Orthography (Spelling-Pronunciation Interface) 191
Exercises 193

Answers to Some Exercises 194

Bibliography 203

Index 206

All about Language

1

1.1 What is Language?

Language is an essential attribute of our life entrusted with the task of defining, interpreting and analyzing the intricacies of human existence. Here, the term 'human existence' has a very wide connotation that includes all non-human components of the universe, as all of these are explained and identified by human efforts only. It would not be an overemphasis to say that all the components of this universe largely owe their existence to language as it is language through which their distinct identity is established in the vast pattern of creation. From this perspective, the domain of language becomes so extensive that an attempt aimed at defining it in a satisfactory manner appears to be a big challenge to our intellect. Linguists have made serious efforts in the direction of defining it, but most of the definitions have failed to capture the whole panorama of language. In a true sense, the inter-relationship between language and human life is so pervasive that encompassing it with words seems to be an elusive attempt. Let us have a look at some of the definitions of language.

1. "Language is a system of conventional spoken and written symbols by means of which human beings, as members of a social group and participants in its culture, communicate."

Encyclopedia Britannica (Vol. 13)

2. "Language is purely human and non-instinctive method of communicating ideas, emotions and desires by means of system of voluntarily produced symbols."

Sapir (1921)

3. "A language is a set (finite or infinite) of sentences, each finite in length and constructed out of a finite set of elements."

Noam Chomsky (1957)

4. "Language is human vocal noise (or the graphic representation of this noise in writing) used systematically and conventionally by a community for purposes of communication."

David Crystal (1989)

5. "Language is a form of human communication by means of a system of symbols principally transmitted by vocal sounds."

R.H. Robins (1990)

Apart from these definitions, there are many other attempts made by the linguists in this direction which are difficult to enumerate.

A sensitive look at these definitions clearly indicates certain common points among them, such as, language is a means of communication; it is symbolic; it is systematic; it is vocal and graphic; it is human; etc. Of course, these are the basic features of language which come out as the gist of these definitions. The central point is that language occupies such a wide dimension in our life that its all inclusive definition is yet to be realized. Here, our concern is not to look into the inadequacies of different definitions of language rather to evolve a very comprehensive picture of language for the sake of better understanding of what it actually is.

Language, undoubtedly, is one of the most precious gifts of God bestowed on all the creatures among whom mankind is supreme. This supremacy of mankind among different life-forms may rightly be attributed to its most developed form of vocal organs which helped mankind develop a very organized system of sounds and symbols that constitute a language. Language must be immensely credited for the advancement of mankind in all walks of life right from the day of its origin up to modern time. It can be evidenced by the fact that the most developed societies usually have the most developed forms of languages. The greatness of any civilization and culture is truly acknowledged by its linguistic richness as history shows that all the great ancient civilizations like Greek, Roman, Egyptian, Indian, etc. had well developed languages.

As soon as we are born, the role of language starts in our life. The weeping of a newly born baby expresses his/her trouble that is the language of a child. Any form of external behaviour shown by an individual is a form of language because of its expressive quality. That means a language may not be all the time phonic or graphic, it may be expressed through gesture or body movement as well. The nodding of our head to express willingness is certainly a form of language. The process of thinking is not possible without language. It would not sound superfluous and insensible to say that every response shown by an individual under the effect of a stimulus is a form of language. The natural response of drawing our hands from fire is a form of language that passes on or expresses the information of unfriendly relationship between fire and our body. On the basis of these observations, it can be said that language is an integral part of our life that is reflected through all those behaviours which tend to express some kind of information.

Language has such an overwhelming influence on life that both of these have become complementary to each other. Language is unimaginable without life, and life is unacknowledged without language. The true nature of life is revealed through language, whereas life is a precondition for the existence of language. Hence, both of these derive their sustenance from each other showing a high degree of inter-dependence. This strong bond between language and life has dramatically expanded the dimension of both. That is to say, the high degree of advancement in life has made language as extensive as life itself.

The very pervading nature of language in life has certainly brought many characteristics to language, in the light of which it may further be understood. Therefore, let us have a look at the characteristics of language.

1.2 Characteristics of Language

On the basis of the role played by language in human life, certain characteristics are commonly observed in it. The listing out of these characteristics will help us in understanding the nature of language. The following characteristics of language may be enumerated.

1. Language is a Medium of Communication: The most important feature of language is that it serves the communicative needs of mankind. We show our feelings, emotions, ideas, and what not with other members of society through language. It does not serve only day to day communication requirements, but also those which are of eternal values, i.e. through literature that passes on from one generation to another. As language serves the communicative needs of mankind in general, there are many common universal concepts among different languages of the world due to which it becomes easier to learn other languages, and it promotes inter-cultural interaction. Today, the whole world appears to be a global village simply because of revolution in the field of communication for which credit should largely go to language. The communicative ability of language has really brought the whole world under one umbrella. It has accelerated the pace of advancement of the modern world in many ways.

2. Language is Symbolic: Any language works with the help of certain symbols or signs. Through these symbols, the different objects of nature or abstractions of life are identified. For example, the word 'book' is treated as a symbol to convey the idea associated with it, i.e. a book is something which has many pages with neatly printed pieces of information. Thus each language operates with specific sets of symbols that represent the various things or aspects, concrete or abstract, found in a specific socio-cultural set-up.

3. Language shows Arbitrariness: It shows arbitrariness in the sense that there is no logical connection between a symbol used and the meaning conveyed through it. That is to say, there is no scientific reason why we call a pen, a pen, not a book. It means that whatever name was given to a particular item of a language by the user of its first generation was decided arbitrarily.

4. Language is Basically Phonic: It is the spoken form of language that gets precedence over all other forms. We have been gifted with well-developed organs of speech that come into use just after we are born. It shows that language is basically phonic. In everyday life as well, the spoken form is the most used form of language. The graphic (written) form may be considered as an offshoot of spoken form that developed in the later phases of human history. There are many languages in the world that still exist in the spoken form only. Therefore, the phonic form is the basic form of language that serves extensively the communicative needs of societies in general.

5. Language is a System of Systems: Any language functions according to certain set of rules. There is a hierarchy of rules which remain operational within the same language. For example, in English language, we have rules involving numbers (singular, plural), person (first, second, third), etc. on one hand, and the rules of subject-verb agreement on the other hand. Likewise, we have rules of the use of different parts of speech. All of these rules come under one heading that is syntax (framing of sentences). Under this syntactic rule, there are prepositional rules, nominal rules, verbal rules, adverbial rules, etc. Therefore, it is seen that there are minor systems embedded inside the major systems, making language a system of systems.

6. Language is Non-instinctive: A child acquires the language that is used in the surrounding in which he/she is brought up. Language is not inherited, and so, it is non-instinctive. A child born to Arabic speaking parents acquires English if this child is brought up in English speaking environment, away from his/her parents.

7. Language is Creative, Modifiable and Elastic: Language is creative in the sense that with finite set of rules we can produce infinite number of sentences. The same idea may be expressed in plenty of ways that would have never been used before by anyone. At the same time, language is subject to change. Modern English is different in many ways from the Old English and Middle English. As change is the rule of society, so is the case with language because language is the expression of society. With the growing dimension of society day by day, language is also acquiring new dimension, simply to cope with the rising demands of new expressions, particularly in the field of science and technology. Hence, language is elastic, expandable. A language shrinks as well when its speakers switch over to a new language under different circumstances and stop using the old one. Many languages have become extinct and many are on the verge of extinction depending on the number of speakers. Therefore, it shrinks as well as expands.

8. Language is Primarily Human: Though animals have their own languages which they use during communication as we find that bees buzz, monkeys hoot, lions roar, etc. this non-human form of language is not as well-developed as human language is. Mankind is really gifted with specially designed organs of speech that work in coordination to produce distinct sounds. Such distinction of sounds is not found among animals. They do not have any organized system of language as we have. Most of the analytical studies regarding language have been carried out on human language only, and so, most of the features of languages in general are the features of human language. That is to say, it is human language that has given ample scope for study of languages in general making language basically human. Because of several inadequacies and practical problems related to the study of animal's language, we have heavily drawn upon human language in terms of its scientific study. Therefore, it can undeniably be said that language is primarily human.

1.3 The Language of Animals

In our daily life, we observe that animals also communicate usually when they encounter a difficult situation in their life. Bees start buzzing when their hive is disturbed; monkeys start hooting when they feel any threat; lions start roaring when they face unconventional situations; cows start mooing when they are hungry or thirsty or their calves are taken away from them. It shows that animals too feel the need of communication like humans but their language lacks the nuances of human language as lies the difference between human and animal life itself. Since a developed and elaborate lifestyle (as human beings have) needs a corresponding form of language that may capture all of its diverse manifestations, human language, in due course, has acquired this dimension. Animals fundamentally lack such life features as they don't have a very organized form of social life, a bundle of aspirations, longevity, aesthetic sense, etc. which are the hallmarks of human life. Such differences in life features between humans and animals may partly be attributed to the differences in forms of their languages. It can be evidenced by the fact that there are human communities still in existence which don't have a very well developed form of life and likewise the language. Animal language exhibits some distinct characteristics compared to human language that can be enumerated in the following ways.

(a) Animal language is not as well organized as human language is. Since animals don't have a developed set of organs of speech like that of humans, they are unable to produce different varieties of speech sounds. It is mostly invariable and non-discrete, i.e. we cannot identify separate sound units in continuous speech of animals. This non-discrete sound feature poses a serious challenge to linguistic research on animals.

(b) Animal language does not cross the limit of time and space unlike human language that crosses. From this angle, animal language is highly localized, confined to a very small area depending on the loudness of speech. Moreover, it cannot be carried on up to the coming generations unlike human languages which appeal to the posterity through books, compact discs, movies, etc.

(c) Animal language is predominantly instinctive in nature as animals inherit their languages as a result of genetic endowment, whereas human language is acquired depending on the environment one is brought up in. The experiments carried on chimpanzees named Viki, Chimpsky, Washoe, etc. who were brought up with human beings for a very long period but failed to acquire human language, have given ample hints of this fact.

(d) Animal language is inelastic, non-modifiable and largely monotonous unlike human languages. Because of the predominant monolithic feature of sounds produced by animals, there is hardly any scope of modulation in their speech that may be attributed to such linguistic features.

(e) Animal language does not exhibit two levels of operation in speech production, i.e. among animals, non-discrete sounds are produced in a continuum where the difference between individual sounds and their combinations in the form of words is not realized. Contrastively, in the case of human language, individual sounds which are discrete and meaningless, are put together in different combinations in the form of words which are meaningful units. This becomes a dual operation in the sense that firstly, meaningless units in the form of sounds are produced, and secondly, they are placed in suitable combinations in the form of words that give meanings.

On the basis of the aforementioned facts about the animal language, it can be said that animal language is a highly under-developed form of language compared to the human language. Actually, the vocal tracts of animals are designed in such a way that they cannot produce clearly distinguishable sound units. This is a serious limitation among animals that does not let their language develop like human beings.

1.4 Difference between Language and a Language

When we talk about the medium of communication of the whole human race, it is 'language' in general, that is universal phenomenon of human society. On the other hand, when we talk about the medium of communication of a particular society which has one language, we are surely talking about 'a language'. To clarify it further, the term 'language' is used to indicate that common linguistic characteristic of human being which it possesses as a member of human race, whereas the term 'a language' is used to indicate that common linguistic characteristic of human being which it possesses as a member of a particular social group. Thus 'language' is specific to human race, whereas 'a language' is specific to a particular society of human race. As a member of human race we acquire 'language' but as a member of a particular society we acquire 'a language' that is specific to this society only, such as, Arabic is a language specific to Arab society.

1.5 The Functions of Language

The most obvious function of language is to fulfil the communicative needs of mankind. But this communication is multi-faceted and varied.

Apart form working as a tool of direct communication, language serves many other functions that may be enumerated as follows:

1. On the basis of the language used by an individual we come to know about his/her socio-cultural and even educational background as the language of a taxi driver differs in many ways from the language of a professor. Hence, it functions as a tool of identification.

2. Language reveals the psychology and above all the personality of an individual even though he/she does not speak about his/her psychology or personality. The way a speaker uses language discloses his/her inner-self. This function of language proves to be very helpful in identifying the anti-social elements, especially when they are interrogated in police custody.

3. Language transmits culture from one generation to another through various means. Since culture is largely manifested through language, it is carried on to posterity in written forms through literature. Today, we know about our ancient cultural traits basically due to the availability of some texts that portray the contemporary culture in details. Many religious texts are the main sources that enlighten the current generation about the grandeur of past in totality transmitting a strong belief system that by and large sustains a society. Language, thus, plays a very vital role in this act of transmission.

4. Language encourages inter and intra-cultural activities, and thus, strengthens inter-human relationship. Modern world is a good example of it. People are migrating to different parts of the world leading to the expansion of inter-cultural activities. This inter-mixing of cultural traits has increased partly with the growth of translation and the emergence of global languages like English that highly facilitates this practice.

5. Language shows the state of advancement of any society in all respects. A developed language is a distinction of a developed society. The material prosperity and the aesthetic exuberance are the hallmarks of excellence of an advanced society which can't be realized without a fully developed language. So, language functions as a vital agency that executes the realization of overall richness of a society.

6. The different forms of language such as music, dance, caricature, etc. work as the source of entertainment for mankind.

Thus, it is seen that language renders many kinds of valuable services to mankind in addition to its well established function of fulfilling all sorts of communicative needs.

Exercises

Answer these questions.

Q1. What do you mean by language? What is the difference between language and a language?

Q2. What are the important characteristics of language? Describe in detail.

Q3. How is animal language different from human language?

Q4. What are the functions of language?

Q5. How can you say that language is a system of systems? Substantiate it with examples.

Q6. What is the relationship between language and society?

The World of Linguistics

2

2.1 What is Linguistics?

Linguistics is that branch of knowledge which attempts to make a scientific study of language. Here the term scientific implies a well-organized, comprehensive and systematic study of language. We know that every language has certain systems that make it operational under specific circumstances. Linguistics analyses these underlying systems of language in order to describe their distinctive features. Each language is identified with a set of sounds, letters, words, sentences and meanings, etc. which are its constituents. All of these constituents work in accordance with certain rules to produce the desired meaning which is the ultimate goal of a language. Linguistics brings to light the inherent link among these different constituents of a language and evolves theories regarding its functioning. It takes into account all the possible features of a language that can be correlated with its expressive potential. Linguistics strives to present a very objective picture of language but at the same time it does not become oblivious of its subjective implications. Now let us look at the observation of R.H. Robins. He says:

> Linguistics is concerned with human language as a universal and recognizable part of the human behaviour and of the human faculties perhaps one of the most essential to human life as we know it, and one of the most far reaching of human capabilities in relation to the whole span of mankind's achievements.

This observation considers linguistics as an area of enquiry into the realm of language that is a universal characteristic of human beings. That is to say, linguistics basically deals with the characteristics of languages in general regardless of the characteristics of a particular language. To be more specific, linguistics looks at language with a broad perspective, and so, adopts an all inclusive approach in its analysis and description. It does not study only the mechanism operational behind language rather takes into account all the sociological and psychological factors that have considerable bearing on it. Undoubtedly, there is a proven link between language and society, and it is studied in detail in linguistics. Further, how a language is acquired and learnt is the field of exploration for linguistics. Moreover, linguistics comes out with the ways of contrasting two languages at different levels and puts forward the similarities and dissimilarities between them that help in understanding the general nature of these languages. On the basis of these contrastive studies, certain theories regarding the learning and teaching of these languages are evolved. Thus, linguistics makes a thread-bare analysis of all the ingredients of language in a scientific manner, and postulates theories regarding its different aspects. Further, it attempts to explore new dimensions of language as we have computational or cyber linguistics, ethno linguistics, etc. today.

Based on the aforesaid observations, it can be said that linguistics is a very comprehensive, extremely analytical and an ever growing field of knowledge that intends to explain the intricacies of language in entirety.

2.2 The Scientific Nature of Linguistics

Conventionally, any study which is carried on in a systematic and rational manner is considered to be scientific. From this perspective, the study of all subjects regardless of the stream (science, social sciences, and humanities) is treated as scientific. But it does not mean that the distinction between natural sciences and social sciences in terms of their ways of study has come to an end. There are certain fundamental factors associated with a particular kind of study that make it purely scientific. These factors may be enumerated as:

(a) the requirement of laboratory for experiments,
(b) the reliability of result after experiments,
(c) the value-neutrality of result,
(d) the uniformity of output (result) with a particular kind of input,
(e) the use of technical devices in conducting the experiment,
(f) the reliability of data collected for experiment, and
(g) the degree of dependence on inductive method of conducting an experiment, etc.

In the course of studying a subject if these factors are commonly observed, such a study is purely scientific. In the case of studying linguistics, most of these factors are taken into account such as, language lab equipped with modern devices like computer, audiometer, microphone, oscillograph, pitchmeter, recorders, etc. is used for conducting experiment. The result of the experiment is predominantly objective and hence value-neutral. Usually inductive method is preferred for research in which the final statement or outcome of research is released only after the completion of all the procedures right from the observation and collection of data, their interpretation, formation of hypothesis to the final result.

To make it more clear, we can consider an experiment that tends to find out the total number of sounds used in a language.

First of all, the speech of a particular number of speakers is recorded, then it is analyzed and at last a statement is released that is usually value-free, objective and verifiable. The repetition of this experiment is bound to give the uniform result if all the procedures have been adopted in the right manner. This clearly indicates the predominantly scientific nature of linguistics. On this basis it can be said that linguistics is like pure sciences.

But taking into account the variety of research conducted in linguistics and its widening dimension, it is observed that there are many branches of linguistics like psycholinguistics (acquisition of language), sociolinguistics (language in relation to society), etc. in which purely scientific study is not possible. Such branches have a lot of variables at different levels, and so, the possibility of getting a value-free, objective and precise result is rare. Linguistics tends to become like social sciences in such cases because of its dependence on deductive method of study, variation in result, predominantly subjective nature of data collected for study, etc. For example, when a research is conducted to find out the degree of social recognition attached to a particular language, it is difficult to undertake such a work in the manner pure sciences are dealt with because of the factors cited above. Hence, it is seen that linguistics as a discipline shows the characteristics of pure science as well as social science. The spoken and written form of language treated objectively in the course of study brings linguistics close to natural science, whereas the part of linguistics that deals with derivation of meaning from spoken and written forms, and their implications in different ways in a socio-cultural set-up, leads it close to social sciences.

To sum up, an attempt is made in linguistics to make the study of language scientific by incorporating all the possible components of science in it, but the deep and intricate relationship of language with society eludes linguistics to be purely scientific. Hence, linguistics may rightly be placed as an intermediary between pure science and social science.

2.3 Scope of Linguistics

As we know that every field of knowledge requires language for its expression, and linguistics deals with analysis and description of language, so the scope of linguistics is very extensive. The advancement of modern civilization is further contributing to the expansion of dimension of linguistics because of addition of new information to the existing state of knowledge.

Linguistics studies languages from utilitarian, social, historical, psychological, physiological and above all human perspectives. It means linguistics studies language:

(a) in terms of its utility as a medium of communication (utilitarian),
(b) as an agent of initiating any change in society at different levels (social),
(c) as an evidence of our past (historical),
(d) as the reflector of our behaviour (psychological),
(e) as a product of certain physical activity (physiological), and
(f) as a specific attribute of mankind (human).

This description is an attempt to encapsulate the wide range of language that is as extensive as our imagination may go. It is relevant to mention here that imagination is possible only through language. As we cannot imagine without language, so whatever comes within the purview of imagination, becomes the subject matter of linguistics.

Linguistics starts with the description of the smallest units of language that are sounds (phonic) and letters (graphic), and it goes up to the level of discourse analysis. It makes classification after classification (taxonomic approach) of different components of language and tries to give a rational interpretation of the systems underlying it. The whole corpus of study of language under linguistics can be divided into three sections—historical, comparative and descriptive. The historical study focuses on the historical facts related to a language such as, the point and place of its origin, changes in it with passage of time, etc. The comparative study takes into account certain common features found among languages and postulates theories based on these common points. The descriptive study focuses on describing each and every feature of language in a systematic manner. Modern linguistics is basically descriptive in nature.

Looking at the way linguistics studies language, it can be said that the range of linguistics is very wide and day by day it is getting wider because of the emergence of new fields like Computational linguistics, Anthropological linguistics, Philosophical linguistics, etc.

Considering the fact that language is a precondition for any discipline to exist in academic world, linguistics creates the scope for itself. This has really resulted into the ever-expanding dimension of linguistics.

2.4 Levels of Linguistic Analysis

As we have come to know that linguistics studies languages in a scientific and analytical manner, it takes into account the smallest as well as the largest unit that constitutes a language. Any language is made up of basically two kinds of material-sound and letter. These are the elementary items, the raw materials that make a language. These sounds and letters are the indivisible items which are combined to produce bigger units of a language. Therefore, linguistics starts with the minimal distinct sound that is the smallest unit of a language in speech form. These sounds in different combinations produce words and sentences used in speech.

Likewise, a letter is the minimal distinct unit of a language in written form. These letters make words, words make sentences, and sentences produce meaning. It is seen that a language has a set of systems working at different levels, that is to say, at the level of sounds, letters, words, sentences, and meaning.

Linguistics studies languages at each of these levels which can be seen through this chart.

Components of language	**Levels of study**
Sound	phonetics/phonology
Letter	graphology
Word	morphology
Sentence	syntax
Meaning	semantics

The level of study at which the sounds of language are described, analyzed and classified, is called phonetics. Under this heading, we study about the production of sounds, their transmission and reception.

The study of sounds of a particular language is done under the heading phonology. How different sounds of a language are produced; what organs are involved in the production of these sounds; what is the quality of these sounds?, etc. all of these matters are discussed in detail in phonology. The written form of language has letters as the smallest unit. Graphology studies the letters or the writing system of a language. How different symbols are used in graphic form to convey a particular kind of visual perception constitutes the subject matter of graphology. Morphology deals with the study of words. How words are formed, how prefixes and suffixes affect the meaning of words, and how different morphemes, the smallest grammatical units of a language, are identified, etc. constitute the subject matter of morphology.

Syntax deals with the structure of sentences. A sentence is the largest structural unit of a language in the sense that it conveys the complete meaning. A sentence is formed with the application of different rules of grammar working as system inside the system. So, syntax analyses different systems working behind the formation of sentences. It describes in detail the different components of a sentence and the role played by them in derivation of meaning. It proposes a very scientific classification of different constituents of a sentence. Semantics studies the meanings of words and sentences of a language. It analyses different contexts in which the meaning of words changes. It deals with meaning in respect of change in the grammatical category of words as well. Pragmatics talks about the ways meaning can be derived from an utterance (verbal expressions), i.e. taking into account the intention of the speaker. Pragmatics is considered as an extension of semantics by many linguists. Lexicology deals with the proper study of vocabulary of a language, i.e. the way dictionaries are prepared on the basis of lexical features.

These are the fundamental levels of linguistics at which the study of different elements of language is undertaken. They constitute the theoretical basis for linguistic studies. Language is studied at these levels in a matter of fact way following an entirely objective approach. Since the study of language at these levels provides theoretical basis to linguistics, all of these studies are incorporated under the heading Theoretical linguistics. The justification of the term theoretical lies in its application potential, i.e. a theory derives its sustenance from its application. The findings of theoretical linguistics are applied in language teaching, translation studies, contrasting languages, etc. Such applications have led to the emergence of Applied linguistics as another level of linguistic studies. The area of applied linguistics has grown wide today due to the inclusion of new fields of study like discourse analysis, language acquisition, semiotics, etc. Since language is a very vast entity that can easily be associated with many facets of our life, its domain is constantly expanding with enlargement of the scope of scientific enquiry. The emergence of areas like forensic linguistics, computational linguistics, neurolinguistics, ethnolinguistics, etc. is its clear indication. These new areas of linguistics are highly interdisciplinary in nature. On the basis of the aforesaid description, it sounds reasonable to divide the whole corpus of linguistic studies into two parts—micro-linguistics and macro-linguistics. All linguistic studies which are undertaken at minute levels conforming to the standards of pure science, i.e. with utmost objectivity, value neutrality, and theoretical basis, etc. are considered as micro-linguistics. Language is studied with a broader perspective as well, when it is looked upon in relation to other branches of knowledge, such as psychology, sociology, anthropology, etc. Today we have psycholinguistics, sociolinguistics, stylistics, etc. as the branches of linguistics, which are studied under the heading macro-linguistics. Thus, this classification of macro- and micro-covers the whole range of linguistic analysis. Micro-linguistics is objective, theoretical, and value neutral, whereas macro-linguistics is subjective, applied, and vulnerable to values of life. The study of language is carried on at all of these levels.

2.5 Major Branches of Linguistics

Linguistics has now well established itself as an autonomous area of study in the world of academia. Its relevance has further increased with revolution in the field of information technology that considerably accelerated the pace of globalization. This wave of globalization has promoted inter-lingual interaction. Since language plays a crucial role in connecting people from all across the globe, the interest in learning languages has commonly increased among people world over under the effect of instrumental as well as integrative motivation. Instrumental motivation encourages a learner to learn a language that helps in shaping his/her professional career. Integrative motivation generates interest in a learner who learns a language mainly to know the culture or people of other social set-up.

Linguistics deals with the ways of learning new languages; it talks of different methods of teaching and learning languages; it describes languages in a very systematic manner, and therefore, it proves to be of immense help for anyone interested in learning a new language. It has truly increased the popularity and importance of linguistics today. The components of micro-linguistics, particularly phonetics, morphology, syntax and semantics are very helpful in the conceptualization of objective aspects of a language. On the other hand, macro linguistics includes all other aspects of language that helps us know the different facets of life in a better way, that is to say, how language helps in understanding different branches of knowledge like sociology, anthropology, literature, psychology, etc. Though, it is a fact that language is somehow related to almost every field of knowledge, in some cases its impact is very deep. Here, we shall deal with those areas of knowledge where this impact is so deep that it has led to the emergence of new branches of linguistics. Let us have a look at some of these major branches of linguistics.

2.5.1 Sociolinguistics

It is that branch of linguistics which studies language in relation to society. There is an intimate relationship between language and society. The richness of a language used in a particular society expresses to a great extent the state of development of that society. On the basis of language used by a particular community or an individual, the social status of that community or person is acknowledged. Moreover, a society is classified on the basis of language used in it, i.e. language plays a defining role in social stratification. The upper most stratum of a society that is constituted by usually well-educated people, uses the most refined form of a language. On the other hand, the lower most stratum that is usually the mass of uneducated people uses the dialectal form of a language. A refined form of language may be marked with standard use of vocabulary, well-formed sentences and proper accent, etc. whereas a dialectal form of language exhibits considerable deviations from grammatical rules in the framing of sentences, the use of substandard vocabulary like slangs and colloquial expressions, and unmarked accent, etc. The people of lower class try to imitate the speech of the people of upper class whenever they get a chance as they think language to be a medium of upward social mobility. The difference between the language of masters and slaves has always been a social reality. In India, the fascination for speaking English can be seen among the majority of people that can largely be attributed to our colonial status. Sociolinguistics studies the different features of languages from all these perspectives. The governments take many decisions based on the number of speakers of a particular language. These decisions start affecting other linguistic communities and a kind of polarization is triggered driven by linguistic factors. It is a very common phenomenon in a multilingual society like India that has witnessed such polarizations at many occasions since independence. In the determination of language policy of a plurilingual nation, a government encounters a lot of challenges. A scene of clash of interests among different linguistic groups emerges and it unleashes disturbing waves in social harmony.

Further, sociolinguistics studies about the relationship between language and culture. Language that is an integral part of culture determines cultural traits of a particular race or tribal community. What linguistic features define the cultural traits of such a community is studied under the heading Anthropological linguistics. Truly, the standardization of a tribal language is construed largely as a movement towards the civilizational advancement of a tribal community. This sociolinguistic phenomenon exists extensively throughout the world which is a living topic for sociolinguistics. Moreover, the emergence of English speaking community cutting across the geographical boundary is a remarkable development that presents a good example of sociolinguistic interplay. In modern globalized set-up, English is acknowledged as a global language and English speaking people are identified as global citizens. Thus, language and society are intricately related and investigation of this intricacy constitutes the subject matter of sociolinguistics.

2.5.2 Psycholinguistics

It is that branch of linguistics which studies the relationship between language and mind. All linguistic behaviours are the reflections of certain mental operations as mind is the regulator of all of our activities. What mental operations occur when we use language; which part of our brain remains active to produce the desired linguistic effect; and how we acquire and learn language, etc. are the subject matter of psycholinguistics. When we use a language either in spoken or written form, certain mental exercise takes place. Usually speech is preceded by thinking and so it can be said that the process of speech starts in mind. Therefore, mind plays a very important role in realization of language in any form. It is an area of linguistics in which much research work is underway. The part of psycholinguistics which studies the physical features of our brain in order to establish a correlation between language and specific organ of brain is called neurolinguistics. We have made considerable advancement in finding out some areas in our brain which are accountable for certain linguistic behaviours. For instance, Broca's area located in the left hemisphere of our brain is associated with the production of speech. Moreover, we find many people suffering from linguistic disorders, such as aphasia (difficulty in understanding), amnesia (loss of memory), and dyslexia (difficulty in reading), etc. which have roots in our brain. It gives ample evidence of close connection between language and brain. A damage caused to our brain may lead to any linguistic disorder.

Psycholinguistics acquired a new dimension after the advent of Noam Chomsky to the arena of linguistics in the second half of the 20th century, who came out with some revolutionary theories regarding language acquisition. He proposed that we are born with exceptional language learning ability. He gave the concept of Universal Grammar that accounts for the universal features of languages in general. Any language used in the world functions with some of the features of this universal grammar, i.e. no language contains any feature that is not present in universal grammar. Therefore, it becomes very easy for children to pick up linguistic items of their mother tongue as these remain embedded in their mind in the form of constituents of universal grammar. Further, psycholinguistics also takes into account the social factors that come to the way of language acquisition and learning. Further, in the course of learning a language, especially in the adulthood, certain psychological factors like anxiety, stress and tension, etc. exercise profound effect on learning. All of these are studied minutely under this heading. Thus, psycholinguistics includes in its fold cognitive as well as social factors that have direct or indirect bearing on language acquisition and learning.

2.5.3 Stylistics

It deals with the linguistic analysis and interpretation of a text, i.e. a text is analyzed in terms of linguistic features like phonological, morphological, syntactic and lexico-semantic, etc. Any text exhibits these linguistic features with variation in style only that makes a writer or a text distinct. On the basis of these linguistic features, we classify different kinds of texts, such as literary, journalistic, scientific, etc. For instance, a literary text is marked by the use of literary devices like figures of speech that makes it indirect and connotative, whereas a text of science shows the direct use of language that is denotative where objective is simply to pass on information to the readers.

Stylistics attempts to employ the statistical method in analysis of a text, i.e. it takes into account the numeral approach like the number of different kinds of syllables, words, and sentences, etc. used in a text. It looks at a text in an extremely objective way so as to come out with the most accurate judgement in its evaluation. Wales reasonably defined stylistics as "a discipline that is principally concerned with describing the formal features of texts and the functional significance of these features in relation to the interpretation of the text". To elaborate it further, each formal (linguistic) feature has some specific function, and this relationship is encoded in a text to produce meaning. Stylistics endeavours to decode this relationship in a verifiable manner.

Stylistics has proved to be very helpful in developing a proper understanding of a text. Its findings in terms of derivation of meanings of a text are much reliable because it considers only the physically verifiable facts, the linguistic data as the parameters for making a judgement. It gives remarkable insights and significant clues to the readers in deciphering the meanings of texts, especially literary in nature. In a text of judiciary, the awareness of stylistic features controls a reader in making misinterpretations of the rules. Moreover, it attempts to investigate the imprint of individualism in writings and the effect that it creates on the readers. Thus, this branch of linguistics attempts to equip a reader with reliable linguistic tools that guide him/her in exploring the possible semantic range of a text.

2.5.4 Applied Linguistics

As the name implies, it deals with the application of theories advocated by pure linguistics in the areas like language teaching, contrastive studies, translation, and many other newly emerging domains such as culture, international studies, media studies, etc. The first half of the 20th century is marked by the dominance of structuralists like Saussure and Bloomfield in linguistics. Since structure was in the centre of activity, the new methods of teaching language were also based on structure. While teaching language, the structure of mother tongue was put side by side with the structure of the target language, i.e. the contrastive method of teaching language was preferred. The tradition of contrasting two languages influenced language teaching as well as translation. The pattern practice became very popular, and the concept of positive and negative transfer from the mother tongue into the target language evolved. All these linguistic trends became the subject matter of applied linguistics. In the initial phases of development, therefore, applied linguistics drew its sustenance from basically three domains—language teaching, contrastive studies and translation, and all of these still continue to be the major stuff for it.

In the last few decades, applied linguistics has considerably widened its horizon by taking into its fold a large spectrum of human activity. Language that is endowed with defining potential of an individual or entity can easily be associated with any domain especially on which its influence is vividly observed. Such domains are society, culture, literature, politics, gender, media, etc. which stand in a very close relationship with language. Applied linguistics studies about this relationship in much details under the headings sociolinguistics, ethnolinguistics, stylistics, discourse analysis, etc. Thus, applied linguistics is covering new strides these days and further inclusions are likely. The observation of Fairclough is very relevant in this context—"The challenge to applied linguistics is to reshape its tradition in engaging with and trying to operationalize new thinking about language including poststructuralist and postmodernist thinking in new ways of analyzing languages".

2.6 The Relevance of Studying Linguistics

As every field of knowledge has its own significance that may be attributed to its existence, linguistics is also not an exception. Its importance as a discipline of serious academic enquiry is growing fast today as it has proved to be a very useful tool in addressing the communicative needs of present globalized set up. Today's world has changed into a village under the influence of globalization necessitating inter-cultural migrations. The revolution in the field of information-technology can solely be credited for this rapid growth of globalization. Since this information-technology is largely based on languages, the importance of a field that scientifically studies languages can easily be understood. This inter-cultural penetration encourages the tendency of learning new languages in which linguistics proves to be of much help. As we know that linguistics postulates theories regarding the learning of languages, people get more interested in it. A linguist knows about the inner mechanism involved in the working of a language, and this information helps him in formulation of methods of learning and teaching languages.

Contrastive linguistics evolves the ways of comparing languages that makes, in turn, a learner aware of the similarities and differences existing between a new language and the mother tongue. This awareness becomes very helpful in learning the new language. For instance, a learner of English with Hindi as his mother tongue comes to know about the structural difference between English (S+V+O) and Hindi (S+O+V) sentences with the help of contrastive linguistics, and it considerably facilitates his learning. The role of linguistics in language learning and teaching, therefore, is of paramount importance in the present global set-up. Further, in the field of translation which has also become very important these days due to inter-cultural interaction, linguistics plays a crucial role. A linguist can definitely work as a good translator or interpreter as he knows the nuances of languages. A scientific and comprehensive idea of languages certainly helps in the making of a good translator. Again in developing the software of language, the knowledge of linguistics becomes very important. Stylistics facilitates our understanding of literary nuances of a text to a very large extent. It helps us in developing an insight into the meaning features of a text which is largely reliable. Historical linguistics gives us an inkling of the state of a language in past that gives us an idea of the modifications taking place in a language under various conditions with passage of time. It becomes useful in classifying the difficult and easy linguistic features of a language on the basis of changes that occur in it with its onward journey. All the areas discussed above have been traditionally associated with linguistics where its relevance is well established, and it won't be an overemphasis to claim that this association played a very vital role in emergence of linguistics as an independent discipline with almost universal acknowledgement.

In the last few decades, linguistics has covered new strides to prove its relevance in this fast changing technology-centered world. It has survived the onslaughts of immense consumerist attitude of an ultra-modern world where the fate of a discipline rests on its productivity in terms of fulfilling the growing demands of a highly competitive global society. Linguistics has made its presence felt in film industry by chiselling the art of script and dialogue writing. A linguist proves to be more resourceful in script and dialogue writing as he knows the intricacies involved in the use of language. The use of linguistic skills in writing of advertisement and preparing the text of cartoons can easily be understood. Many linguists are proving their skills in these fields. Journalism is also an area where linguistic resourcefulness matters much. A linguist knows better how to present a text (written or spoken) in the most depersonalized manner, i.e. in a matter of fact way. We are living in a world that is highly sensitive and many a time, controversies are created due to the ambiguous style of writing that may partly be attributed to the lack of linguistic skill of the writer. Here comes the significance of a linguist who can considerably minimize such problems, especially in media.

Transliteration is another area where linguistic skill plays a crucial role. With fast spread of knowledge in almost all spheres of life cutting across the geographical boundaries, the need of transliteration is much felt. The linguistic diversity at global level provides much scope to transliteration that flourishes in many fields, especially in medical profession where the names of medicines and instruments are usually transliterated for the sake of convenience in use. A linguist can surely do more justice to this task than anyone else. The use of linguistics in language pathology or speech therapy is getting much popularity. The number of people with speech defects is increasing and a speech therapist with sound footing in linguistic skills performs well in eradicating such defects. In the field of cryptography, a linguist proves to be of much importance as he knows about the components of words in terms of sounds, syllables, and morphemes, the smallest units. A linguist can, therefore, identify and analyze the different parts of an unknown language in a better way, and decipher the encoded messages. Cryptography is widely used in intelligence and military services where the information of linguistics as an input can amply enhance the quality of such services.

Moreover, the emerging domains of applied linguistics are acquiring new horizons adding to the quality of life in general. The revelations brought out by the studies of such domains have largely enabled us to understand life in a much better and comprehensive manner. The growing popularity of linguistics at global level at present may rightly be attributed to its utility in the services of masses. Its inclusion as an autonomous discipline in the syllabi of most of the universities of the world also stands a reliable witness to its relevance for modern society. Since language defines the identity of all sorts of existences in this vast pattern of creation, a discipline entrusted with the task of studying language itself in a scientific way will never lose its sheen and lustre.

Exercises

Q1. What do you mean by the term linguistics?
Give some definitions and explain them.

Q2. Do you consider linguistics a scientific study of language?
Justify your opinion with the help of illustrations.

Q3. Explain the scope of linguistics in modern age.

Q4. What do you mean by the levels of linguistics?
What are these levels and what is their importance in the study of linguistics?

Q5. What are the major branches of linguistics? Explain them.

Q6. Explain the difference between these terms:
(a) Inductive and Deductive method
(b) Psycholinguistics and Sociolinguistics
(c) Phonetics and Phonology
(d) Morphology and Syntax
(e) Integrative and Instrumental motivation

Q7. Why do we study linguistics?

A Brief History of Linguistics

3

Language has been the subject of interest for mankind since the olden days. It can be traced back to the time written records are available in our history. But the phase of sincere enquiry into the sphere of language starts with the work of a great Indian scholar Panini (around 400 B.C.) who gave a detailed description of Sanskrit grammar in his book 'Astadhayayi'. Later on, the great Greek scholar Plato (around 300 B.C.) followed by some Roman scholars came out with such texts of Greek and Roman languages which may be considered as the foundation stone of modern linguistics. Here, we shall take into account the path linguistics has undertaken since its inception to the present day.

3.1 The Approach of Classical Schools of Thought

The pioneer work in the direction of analysis and description of a language was done by Panini, the great Indian scholar, who wrote extensively about the grammar of Sanskrit language. Bloomfield, the great American linguist, has appreciated Panini's grammar as "one of the greatest monuments of human intelligence, which describes in minute detail every inflection, derivation and composition and every syntactic usage of its author's speech. No other language to this day has been so perfectly described". Panini described the rules of word formation, minimal grammatical structure and the concept of inflections. He talked of the relationship between noun and verb of a sentence, and the placement of words in a sentence so as to give the appropriate meaning. Panini's grammar was further explained by Patanjali, who was also a great Indian scholar. Patanjali wrote 'Mahabhashya' in which he described the sounds of Sanskrit along with the concept of pitch, vowel length, syllable, etc.

These works of Sanskrit language can definitely be regarded as a major step in the foundation of linguistics.

Almost parallel to Indian school, some Greek scholars also showed keen interest in the analysis of Greek language. Plato (427-347 B.C.) was the first Greek scholar whose work 'Cratylus' dealt with the origin of words. Plato tried to find out the logical connection between the properties of the things and their names. Dionysius, Thrax, Apollonius and Potagorus are the other Greek grammarians whose works dealt with etymology, phonetics and grammar. These grammarians described parts of speech, inflections, gender, case, etc. They considered nouns and verbs as the integral parts of a sentence. The concept of subject and predicate was evolved by them. The definition of a sentence as a group of words that gives complete meaning was given by the Greek grammarians. This definition still holds importance.

The tradition established by the Greek grammarians was followed by the Roman grammarians who described Latin language in terms of parameters evolved by the Greek. Donatus (400 A.D.) and Priscian (500 A.D.) were the two important Roman grammarians who wrote Latin grammar that was important for the learners of Latin as well as for the explanation of language in general. These Latin grammarians recognized interjection as a separate word category. They brought about some modifications in the description of grammatical terms given by the Greek. The morphological features of words, the aspects of verbs, and the concept of active and passive along with transitive and intransitive distinctions were explained by these Latin grammarians.

Thus, these Indo-Greek and Roman scholars sowed the seed of linguistics by taking into account the various aspects such as, phonological, morphological, syntactic, semantic, etc.

of their languages. Their efforts paved the way for further enquiry into the realm of language by succeeding generations.

3.2 Linguistics through the Middle Ages and Renaissance

After the fall of Roman empire, no significant development is observed in the field of linguistics for a very long time. Of course, the Latin grammar of Priscian and Donatus remained in use for teaching and learning purposes. During the 13th century, speculative grammar came in vogue with the efforts of catholic philosopher St. Thomas Aquinas. This grammar attempted to provide theoretical explanation or philosophical response to the traditional Latin grammar. The chief aim of these speculative grammarians was to determine the ways we perceive the things when they are referred to as nouns or verbs. That is to say, they formulated the theory to differentiate nouns from verbs, from a different perspective. According to these grammarians a 'book' is a noun and 'walk' is a verb because a book has existence as a physical reality unlike walk. They classified nouns and verbs along with other parts of speech in such a way. Further these speculative grammarians tried to establish the fact that all languages have certain universal characteristics that indicate that they are same in nature at a particular level.

The advent of the great Renaissance that led to revelation of ancient Greek and Roman knowledge infused fresh interest in some scholars to work in the field of language. It was also a period of geographical discovery of a new world by Columbus that necessitated the learning of new languages by the explorers. The invention of 'Printing Press' contributed further in the study of languages. Some scholars paid attention to the inconsistency between spelling and pronunciation that was really a big problem particularly in some languages. A general tendency to compare different languages along with the changes that occurred in them with passage of time developed among the scholars. This work of comparison became easy with the invention of printing press. How changes in the Latin language led to the emergence of French, Italian and Spanish was investigated. The trend of colonization was set in, led by England. By this time, English language had already established itself as one of the important languages. This wave of colonization also necessitated the learning of new languages by the colonizers as well as the colonized. All these scenes entailed an important responsibility on the shoulders of linguists who tried to evolve the tools for contrasting the languages in order to facilitate their learning. The work of Holder entitled 'Element of Speech' is a good example of such an effort in which he dealt with pronunciation. The effort was made by the English scholars to create Universal Phonetic Alphabet that represents the set of symbols for all the sounds used in different languages. An English scholar named William Jones (1747-1794 A.D.) compared Greek, Latin, Gothic and Sanskrit languages and came out with the result that these languages have common origin. Thus, from 15th to 18th century an increased awareness towards linguistic activities is observed that paved the way for further exploration.

3.3 Emergence of Linguistics as a Science in the 19th Century

By the end of the 18th century, philologists started taking much interest in comparative and historical study of languages. They started collecting data from languages, and analyzed them to find out the common points among them. On this basis, the concept of language family emerged. The similarities between Sanskrit and European languages led to the formation of Indo-European family of languages. Grimm's Law proposed the ways in which letters of one language change into another under certain specific circumstances. He gave the concepts—'ablaut' (vowel gradation) and 'umlaut' (vowel change). Towards the end of the 19th century, a school of linguists appeared as neo-grammarians that tried to give scientific basis to the study of languages by emphasizing on collection of data from different languages. These neo-grammarians dealt with phonetics, bilingualism and dialectology in much detail.

The International Phonetic Alphabet (IPA) was published in 1888 A.D. that was essentially an attempt to identify all the sounds used in different languages of the world. The impact of growth of natural sciences during this period is clearly visible on the study of languages that consequently got inclined towards scientific techniques and methods. All these developments prepared the ground for undertaking scientific study of languages in the succeeding periods.

3.4 Structuralism of the First-half of the 20th Century

The beginning of the 20th century is marked by the emergence of Swiss linguist Ferdinand de Saussure, American linguists Edward Sapir and Bloomfield, whose works became the determinants of the nature of linguistics. Under the effect of colonialism, mass international migration was taking place that brought to light many new languages of colonized and colonizer countries. These languages drew the attention of the contemporary linguists who studied them objectively. It means they took into account the sounds, words and sentences of languages which are objectively analyzable and classifiable. This approach was considerably influenced by the behaviourist school of psychology which believed that it is only external behaviour of mankind that can be subjected to valid scientific enquiry. Since language is a form of behaviour, only those aspects of language can be considered suitable for scientific analysis and description which are clearly observable and concrete. This spirit of enquiry led to the growth of structuralism in linguistics.

Ferdinand de Saussure came out with concepts like synchrony and diachrony, langue and parole, syntagmatic and paradigmatic, etc. which basically aim at structural analysis and description of a language. He considered language as a system of systems and tried to establish the inter-relationship among the different constituents of a language working at different levels. The concept of field-work research was taken into linguistics from anthropology, and language was studied from socio-cultural perspective as well by Franz Boaz and Edward Sapir. The study of language became much descriptive in nature because of the emphasis on collection of data in terms of linguistic facts, their analysis and classification.

Bloomfield's famous book *Language* came out with the theory and practice of linguistic analysis. He employed structural approach in this book in identification and classification of the features of sentence structure. He talked of the area of linguistic enquiry as well in this book. Zelling Harris wrote *Methods in Structural Linguistics* that dealt with a general method of analysing language. Bloomfield dominated the linguistic arena in this period by dealing with several fundamental concepts of linguistics. His attempt to define the concepts like phoneme, allophone, morph, morpheme, allomorph, etc. contributed a lot in giving a scientific garb to linguistics as a subject. His concept of 'Immediate Constituents' as the units of sentence structure was certainly a pioneer attempt in the direction of analysis of a sentence and the identification of its meaningful units.

With the efforts of these linguists, the first International Congress of Linguistics was held in 1928 A.D. in which linguistics achieved the status of an independent subject of scientific enquiry. Its domain was also decided here along with the techniques it needed to employ in conducting the study of languages on scientific pattern. Thus the effort of linguists of this period set linguistics on a strong pedestal.

3.5 Cognitivism of the Second-half of the 20th Century

The structuralism had a serious defect that it excluded the inner operation of mind/brain in the analysis and description of language. Under the effect of behaviourism, the role of mind was ignored because of the belief that what goes inside mind cannot be considered as concrete and observable. This serious limitation of the structuralism caught the attention of the great American linguist Noam Chomsky who came out with the idea that psychological aspects must also be given due consideration in dealing with scientific analysis of language. His book *Syntactic Structures* published in 1957 A.D. brought about remarkable changes in the approach of linguistic analysis. He gave the concepts of competence and performance, and through these, he tried to prove the role of mind/brain in speech. He observed that whatever comes out as speech that is performance, doesn't reflect the whole knowledge (competence) of the speaker of this language. There is always a gap between competence and performance, and so, the role of brain should be taken into consideration to realize the comprehensive nature of language. His cognitive (related to mind) approach aims at studying how a language is learnt, how a child learns his mother tongue, whether we are born with some special device to learn language, etc.

Further, Chomsky propounded the theory of Transformational Generative grammar that talks of the generative ability of grammar. He says that grammar of a language should produce all kinds of correct sentences by application of transformational rules (It has been discussed in the chapter syntax in detail). He tried to make the study of linguistics explanatory which was descriptive in nature during the structuralism. To deal with the why of the linguistic elements, he really made it explanatory and added scientificity to its study. By associating linguistics with psychology, Chomsky widened its horizon. The emergence of branches of linguistics like psycholinguistics, socio-linguistics, anthropological linguistics, ethnolinguistics, applied linguistics, etc. is the evidence of it. As a linguist, Chomsky thoroughly dominates the linguistic scene in the 2nd half of the 20th century. There has been an overwhelming influence of Chomskyan linguistic theory on the linguists of this period.

Thus, it is seen that in the whole journey of linguistics right from the ancient period to the modern, considerable changes have occurred in the nature of study. Modern linguistics has already established itself as an important and autonomous area of scientific study.

Exercises

Answer the following questions.

Q1. What has been the contribution of Indo-Greek and Roman schools of thought in the emergence of linguistics?

Q2. What was the impact of Renaissance on linguistics of that period?

Q3. Write a note on the contribution of Ferdinand de Saussure in the emergence of structuralism.

Q4. How can you trace out the influence of behaviourism on structuralism?

Q5. Bring out the major differences between structuralism and cognitivism.

Q6. Make a comparative account of contribution of Bloomfield and Noam Chomsky in the emergence of linguistics as an autonomous field of study.

Q7. What do you mean by Transformational Generative grammar? How has it changed the approach of studying a language?

Major Concepts in Linguistics

4

During the phase of emergence of linguistics as a separate branch of knowledge, many aspects of language needed a scientific and systematic explanation. In the due course some new terminologies appeared to encode certain specific concepts related to language. For the proper understanding of linguistics, it is important to have a clear concept of these terms which are commonly used in dealing with several aspects of this subject. Let us have a look at these concepts.

4.1 Synchrony and Diachrony

The concepts of synchrony and diachrony were given by Ferdinand de Saussure, a Swiss linguist of early 20th century. He considered language as a very comprehensive entity that required distinct approaches for making its study systematic and scientific. Synchrony and diachrony are the two approaches of studying a language. Synchrony, that is also called descriptive linguistics, studies the different aspects of a language existing at a particular point of time. That is to say, in synchronic study, various aspects of a language are described and analyzed without taking into account the historical aspects of it. How a language operates, what are its components that help in operation, and how different components are inter-related and work in harmony within the whole system of language, etc. all these factors are taken into consideration in synchronic study.

On the other hand, diachronic which is also called historical linguistics, studies a language with historical perspective. It takes into account the changes that take place in a language with passage of time. It is a fact that any living language changes under the influence of different kinds of factors while running down the lane of history. In diachronic study, all kinds of changes that occur in a language since its origin are described.

On the basis of the features of these two approaches, it can be said that the synchronic study is more important than the diachronic study in linguistics. It is a fact that the user of a language is concerned with the state of this language which he/she learns or acquires at a particular stage of time. Such a user has nothing to do with the state of this language hundred years back or at any other point of time. Therefore, synchronic study is the preferred choice that interests majority of the linguists. The relationship between these two approaches has been represented through this diagram by Saussure.

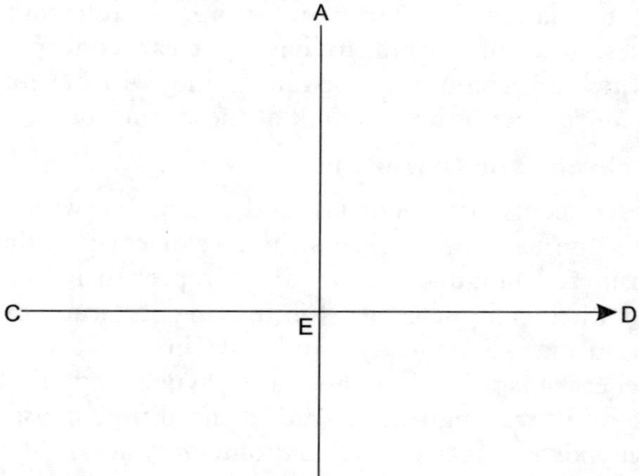

In this diagram 'AB' is the imaginary diachronic axis that indicates the path of a language since its origin. 'CD' is the synchronic axis that intersects 'AB' at point 'E'. It shows the study of a language as it existed at point 'E' in the chain of its history from 'A' to 'B' regardless of its condition at any other point on the axis. This kind of study is synchronic study. On the other hand, the study of a language as it existed at point 'B' in the chain of history in the light of changes that took place in it from the early periods will be considered as diachronic.

4.2 Langue and Parole

It was Ferdinand de Saussure who propounded the concepts of langue and parole. He considered language as a product of a kind of mutual agreement among the members of a society. This agreement is based on the uniform way of looking at different components of a language in order to use it effectively. Because of this agreement at social level, the users of a language get similar kind of impression from different sounds, words, sentences, etc. that constitute this language. Langue as a concept expresses the totality of a language as it exists in terms of words, grammar, pronunciation, and certain other conventions, in the minds of its users. To clarify it further, langue is the sum total of a language used by the members of a society. It is the overall contents of a language embedded in the minds of its users, who constitute a society in which this language is used. So, the nature of langue is predominantly social and abstract.

On the other hand, parole is the physical manifestation of langue, the concrete entity. Parole is realized in terms of actual speech or writing by the users of a language. Langue is the embedded, underlying system of a language in the minds of its users that comes out in the form of parole when this system is used for communication. On this basis it can be said that langue is the legislative side that determines the rules of a language and parole is the executive side that brings these rules to practice. Further, langue is marked by homogeneity because it exists as uniform concepts of different aspects of language in the mind of its users, whereas parole is marked by heterogeneity as the speeches of individuals differ under the effects of several factors. It shows that parole is individual and concrete in nature compared to langue that is social and abstract. Moreover, the mechanism involved in langue is psychological as it works at the mental level only, whereas it is psycho-physical in parole because it works at mental as well as physical level. Langue is the source from which parole is derived.

4.3 Competence and Performance

These concepts were propounded by Noam Chomsky, a modern American linguist. He explained competence as the native speaker's knowledge of his/her language in terms of grammar, vocabulary, pronunciation, etc., whereas performance as the utterance that comes out in real life situations during communication. These concepts are very much similar to the concepts of langue and parole. But the difference between competence and langue is that competence is confined to an individual's knowledge, whereas langue takes into account the whole knowledge of a language shared by its speakers in general. To elaborate it further, competence involves the mastery of rules of language, and performance its application in speech or writing. Competence is free from lapses or slips of memory, while performance is marked by lapses or slips of memory. Therefore, a gap is always observed between competence and performance. In other words, it can be said that competence is a code and performance is its decoding.

It is relevant to mention here that some linguists raise serious doubts about such dichotomies like langue/parole, competence/performance. They argue that these terms are so much interdependent that drawing a sharp line of demarcation between them is not justified. This argument certainly holds water as we know that it is the spoken form of language that is parole or performance that came first in use in our history. With passage of time and advancement of society only, language developed further. From this angle langue or competence has its source in parole or performance. Hence, the degree of interdependence between these terms is so high that these differences cannot be fully validated. But as concepts, these terms and the differences between them are important to keep in mind for the proper understanding of distinct linguistic domains that truly help us in developing an insight into the working of a language.

4.4 Syntagmatic and Paradigmatic Relationship

It was Ferdinand de Saussure who described the structure of a language in terms of two kinds of relationship-syntagmatic and paradigmatic. Keeping in view the fact that language is a very complex organization of different linguistic items like sounds, letters, words, and sentences, etc. which are bound together according to certain rules to produce the desired meaning, Saussure observed that the structure of a language can be explained with the help of two broad relationships that exist among the constituents of a language. Syntagmatic relationship is the horizontal or linear relationship among the different words of a sentence. That is to say, the first word of a sentence stands in syntagmatic relationship with the second word, and it goes on up to the last word. It is a relationship based on the syntactic requirement of a sentence.

On the other hand, paradigmatic relationship is the vertical relationship that exists among the words belonging to the same grammatical class that may be substituted for one another. This relationship is based on the systematic organization of a language. It is a choice relationship also, as many words belonging to the same grammatical class or category exhibit it. For instance, the words like mango, Ali, he, bird, etc. show paradigmatic relationship among themselves as they may be substituted for one another in sentences because of their common belonging to the grammatical class noun or pronoun that usually begins a sentence. It can further be illustrated through these sentences.

SYNTAGMATIC

Ali	is	playing	football	today	**PARADIGMATIC**
They	are	eating	mangoes	slowly	
Birds	are	singing	songs	sweetly	
I	was	beating	him	mercilessly	

Thus, the relationship among the words of each sentence is syntagmatic, that is 'Ali' and 'is' are syntagmatically related to each other, and likewise, 'is' and 'playing' are related, and this sequence continues up to the last word. Again 'Ali' 'they' 'birds' and 'I' have paradigmatic relationship as they all belong to the same functional grammatical class, that is "subject". Likewise, 'playing' 'eating' 'singing' 'beating' show paradigmatic relationship as they all belong to the same grammatical class "verbs". All the tables given above have the sets of words that are in paradigmatic relationship because of their belonging to the common grammatical category or class. The words 'football' 'mangoes' 'songs' 'him' belong to the same grammatical category "object". Likewise the words 'today' 'slowly' 'sweetly' 'mercilessly' belong to the same grammatical class "adverb" showing paradigmatic relationship among themselves. Both of these concepts, syntagmatic and paradigmatic, are useful in the explanation of structures and systems underlying a language.

4.5 Substance and Form

Usually any language works with the help of some phonic (sound) and graphic (written) materials. Certain sets of sounds and letters are used in a particular combination to produce meaningful units of a language. That is to say, a word is a combination of sounds or letters that gives meaning. A particular sound or letter of a language does not bear any meaning. Meaning which is the core of a language comes out only when the sounds or letters take a particular form. Hence, these sounds and letters are the substances, and words and sentences are the forms. A wooden chair is a form and wood is the substance. Substance is the basic building block of a language that produces different forms through which it operates. Substance is the raw material and form is the product. The substances which are phonic and graphic materials are combined according to certain rules to produce meaningful forms. As for example:

Substance	Form
/b/+/æ/+/t/	bat
/r/+/I/+/m/	rim
/m/+/æ/+/n/	man

These sounds make words according to certain linguistic rules of English language. These words are meaningful forms and their constituents, these sounds, separately do not bear any meaning as substance. It shows that a form of a language is a meaningful combination of its substances. Further, it can be said on the basis of these examples that in English language consonant-vowel-consonant combination is usually a meaningful combination that produces forms out of substances.

4.6 Linguistic Sign and Symbol

Any language works with the help of certain sets of signs and symbols. These signs and symbols are physical markers, concrete, and culture-specific as different societies have different sets of signs and symbols for the same thing. This is to say, the same object is named different in different languages. For example, 'water' in English is *maiya* in Arabic, *pani* in Hindi, *jal* in Sanskrit, etc. It shows that different words are used to represent the same object of nature in different societies. The relationship between the sign and symbol, and the object or idea represented by these, is decided by mutual agreement among the members of society where these signs and symbols are used. The members of British society use 'pen' as a sign to represent an instrument used for writing. The nodding of head, movement of hands, etc. are certain signs that help us in communication. On the other hand, there are certain signs which are represented orthographically (written form). Different sounds of a language are represented by different signs. For example, /p/, /b/, /t/, etc. are all orthographic representations, the signs, for different sounds used in English language.

As regards the difference between a sign and a symbol, a sign represents a single associative bond with an object or idea, whereas a symbol represents multiple associative bond with an object or idea. To clarify it further, the word 'green' is a sign that represents a particular colour, but it becomes a symbol when it is used to show prosperity or exuberance. A sign changes into symbol when it holds more than one layer of relationship with the idea that it tends to convey. It can further be said that all symbols are signs but all signs are not symbols. A symbol emerges out of a sign but all signs do not attain the status of symbol. Symbols are usually the culture-specific extensions of signs.

4.7 Signifier and Signified

Any language operates with the help of words. These words are signs or symbols that represent a particular object or idea. The members of a particular social group associate meaning with the words used in their languages. For example, the word 'book' refers to an object consisted of many printed pages. This association between a word and the idea conveyed through it can be technically understood in terms of signifier and signified. A word is a signifier and the idea conveyed through it is signified.

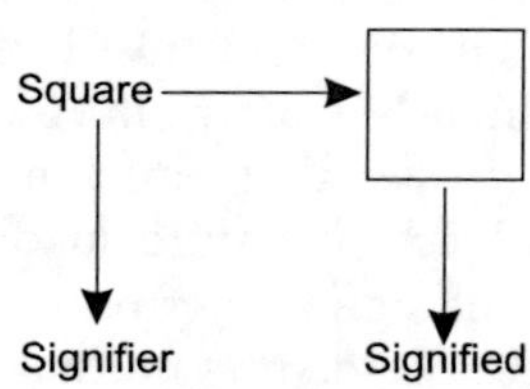

The moment we come across the word square, a particular kind of image of a structure with equal sides comes to our mind. Therefore, what is used as a sign in the form of a word or sound is signifier, and what is conveyed in terms of idea or object is signified.

All the dichotomies mentioned in this chapter are very relevant in understanding certain unique characteristics of language. As linguistics studies a language comprehensively and minutely, it is important to be aware of the differences that exist among these frequently used terms. These terms have given the imprint of scientificity to this discipline. The multi-faceted complex nature of language can be explained in a better way with the help of these terms.

Exercises

Q1. Show the difference between these terms.

(a) Langue and Parole

(b) Syntagmatic and Paradigmatic relationship

(c) Competence and Performance

(d) Sign and Symbol

(e) Signifier and Signified

(f) Synchrony and Diachrony

(g) Langue and Competence

(h) Substance and Form

Q2. How can you say that linguistic signs and symbols are culture specific?

Phonetics

5

5.1 What is Phonetics?

All the languages of the world use certain sets of sounds for the purpose of speech. The individual sounds of languages are combined to produce words. These words are used to produce meaningful sentences or utterances. Though all of these sounds of different languages are produced by almost the same kind of organs of speech, the process of production of these sounds gives them the distinctive features. How a sound is produced, what organs are involved in its production, and what distinctive features this particular sound has got, etc. are the issues taken up in phonetics. It takes into account the way different sounds are transmitted through air from the speaker to the listener along with their reception by the listener. That is to say, phonetics studies scientifically the sounds of human languages in entirety.

The production of speech sound is studied under the heading articulatory phonetics; its transmission is studied under the heading acoustic phonetics; and its reception is studied under the heading auditory phonetics.

All these processes of production, transmission and reception are quite objective in nature, and so, it becomes possible to undertake a scientific study of phonetics. Even scientific instruments are used to measure the amplitude, frequency, pitch, etc. of sounds produced by our organs of speech. Articulatory phonetics describes the role of organs of speech and the mechanism involved in production of speech sounds. Acoustic phonetics deals with the physical properties of sounds during transmission. Auditory phonetics studies the way speech sounds are received with change in their physical properties like loudness, frequency, etc.

In the modern world of globalization, phonetics has become a very important field of study because of growing inter-cultural migration of people. The emerging need of learning new languages induced by international migration has popularized phonetics. It is phonetics that makes a scientific analysis and description of speech sounds of languages, and so, it facilitates the learning of the sounds of the target language. The use of modern scientific devices has made phonetics very interesting and easy as well, a subject to master. It is considerably helpful in understanding the differences existing among the varieties of a language. For example, the differences between British English (R.P.) and American English or Australian English can easily be understood in the light of phonetic description. The discrepancy between spelling and pronunciation existing in some languages is highlighted in phonetics, and it proves to be of much help in developing a clear concept of pronunciation in the concerned languages. Thus, phonetics has emerged as a highly technical and scientific field of study in recent years.

5.2 Speech Production Mechanism

There are certain mechanisms involved in the production of sounds of different languages. These mechanisms are not uniform for all the languages. In majority of the languages of the world, speech is produced through a mechanism called pulmonic egressive. The sounds of English language are also produced through this mechanism. Actually, the air that we inhale goes down to lungs through trachea (windpipe) and it comes out in the form of air-stream through the same channel. The sounds are produced with the help of this air-stream. We can realize it to keep our palm before mouth when we speak. When we want to speak, the walls of lungs contract and it results into pushing the air out. Hence, the muscles of the lung act as initiator of sounds. The air-stream comes out passing through several organs like larynx, pharynx, oral cavity and nasal cavity. During this passage of air-stream from lungs to atmosphere, the organs of speech act in different ways to produce a variety of sounds. Thus, the respiratory tract is used for speech production as well as serving the respiratory function. This mechanism is called pulmonic because the lung is its center and it is egressive because air comes out in the process of speech production. How different sounds of English language are produced through this pulmonic egressive air-stream mechanism will be discussed in the chapter "Phonology".

Apart from pulmonic air-stream mechanism, there are two other important air-stream mechanisms called glottalic and velaric. During the speech when the air is taken in, the process is called ingressive (opposite of egressive). In glottalic air-stream mechanism, closed glottis acts as initiator, and in velaric air-stream mechanism, back of the tongue acts as initiator of sound. The glottalic air-stream produces both egressive and ingressive sounds. The sounds of many African and Indian American languages are produced by glottalic egressive and ingressive air-stream mechanisms. In velaric air-stream mechanism only ingressive sounds are produced such as, in xhosa and zulu, the languages of South Africa. These air-stream mechanisms can further be understood in the light of the role played by each organ of speech in the production of different kinds of sounds.

5.3 The Organs of Speech

There is a certain set of speech sounds operational in any language which is produced through a particular type of air-stream mechanism. Though the air-stream mechanism is the same for one language, the sounds produced vary in quality as we have many sounds in one language. This variation in sounds is caused by different organs involved in production of speech sounds. Here we can see the position of different organs of speech along with their functions. Look at the Fig. 1 that shows the position of these organs.

The Organs of Speech

1-nasal cavity
2-lips
3-teeth
4-alveolar/teeth ridge
5-hard palate
6-velum (soft palate)
7-uvula
8-apex (tip) of tongue
9-blade (front) of tongue
10-dorsum (back) of tongue
11-oral cavity
12-pharynx
13-epiglottis
14-larynx
15-vocal cords
16-trachea (windpipe)
17-esophagus (food pipe)

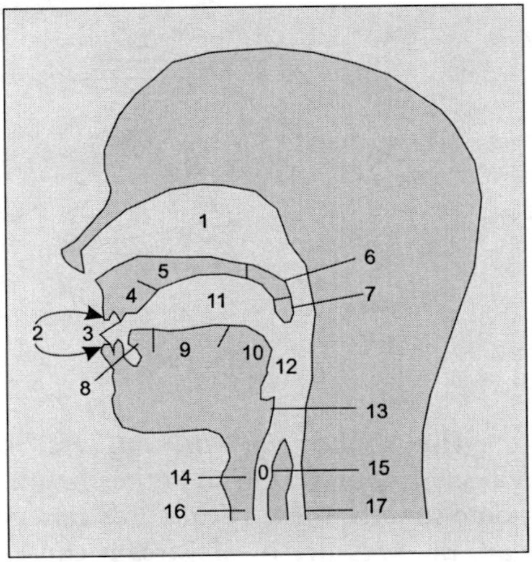

Fig. 1

Now let us describe these organs.

(A) Larynx: The larynx which is also called adam's apple, is situated at the top of the windpipe. Inside the larynx, there remain two thick flaps of muscles, placed horizontally from front to back. They are joined tightly in the front and can be separated at the back. They are called vocal folds or cords (as shown in Fig. 2). The opening between these two flaps is called glottis. These vocal cords can be opened and closed. During the intake of food or water, these vocal cords remain closed to check the entry of the food particles into the windpipe. During normal breathing, vocal cords remain wide apart to give smooth passage to air through glottis. In the production of certain sounds, these vocal cords remain wide apart and air passes out through glottis without any vibration. The sounds produced in this way are called voiceless sounds.

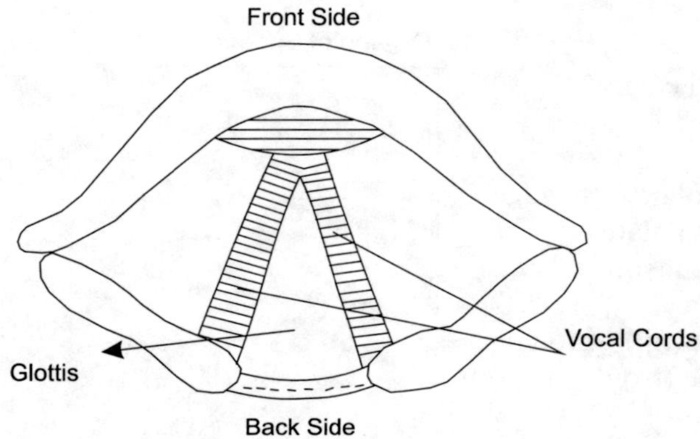

Fig. 2

The sounds /p/, /t/, /k/, etc. of English are therefore voiceless sounds. On the other hand, during the production of some sounds, these vocal cords remain loosely closed, that is to say, the pressure of air-stream causes them to open and close rapidly. It results into the vibration of vocal cords. The sounds produced with the vibration of these vocal cords are called voiced sounds. The sounds /b/, /d/, /g/, etc. of English along with all English vowel sounds are voiced sounds. The vibration of these vocal cords determines the pitch of a sound.

(B) Epiglottis: It is a structure of tissues at the root of the tongue which is lowered during the swallowing of food to prevent it from entering the windpipe.

(C) Pharynx: It is a cavity at the back of the mouth where the passage to the nose, mouth and larynx begins. It has certain roles in articulation of some sounds.

(D) Tongue: It is a very important organ of speech. It is basically divided into three parts: tip, front (blade) and back. Tip is the extreme outer part that remains in touch with teeth ridge in rest position. Front of the tongue is that part which lies opposite the hard palate, and the back is that part which faces the soft palate. All these parts play a crucial role in production of different sounds.

(E) Roof of the Mouth Cavity: It consists of teeth ridge (also called alveolar ridge or alveolum), hard palate, soft palate, and uvula. The teeth ridge is that part which remains just behind the upper teeth, facing the tip of the tongue. It is followed by the hard palate which looks smooth, concave and bony. This hard palate is followed by soft and fleshy soft palate that is called velum also. The last part that follows the soft palate is uvula that remains in hanging position. This velum is flexible and works like a valve in opening and closing of nasal and oral passages for the air-stream in the production of nasal and oral sounds. It can be raised to block the nasal passage and lowered to block the oral passage.

(F) **Teeth:** Teeth are the outermost parts of lower and upper jaw. They are very hard and play an important role in articulation of some sounds in association with tongue or lips. We have sounds /θ/ and /ð/, the initial sounds of the English words 'think' and 'that' which are dental sounds as these are produced with the help of teeth and tongue.

(G) **Lips:** The two lips are the outermost parts of the mouth that work as curtain to mouth cavity. These are very important to block completely the passage of air-stream. Many sounds are produced with the help of lips in association with teeth and tongue. We have sounds like /p/, /b/, /m/, in English which are articulated with the firm contact of both the lips.

These are the organs of speech that produce different kinds of sounds of a language. For proper understanding of distinctive features of sounds of a language, it is important to be aware of the positions of these organs of speech. Now it will be convenient to understand their roles in articulation of different sounds.

5.4 Description of Speech Sounds

A meticulous observation and analysis of sounds produced in a language clearly indicates that the whole set of sounds may be divided into two broad categories: consonants and vowels, depending upon the obstruction caused at some points in the passage of the air-stream. The consonant sounds are those during the articulation of which either complete or partial closure (narrowing) takes place in the passage of the air-stream for a recognizable moment of time. On the other hand, vowel sounds are produced without any obstruction in the passage of air-stream. We can realize it to pronounce these two kinds of sounds. Take for example the consonant sounds: /p/, /t/, /k/, /s/, /l/, /r/, etc. during the articulation of these, either complete closure (in case of /p/, /t/, /k/) or partial closure (in case of /s/, /l/, /r/) takes place as a result of two organs of speech coming firmly in contact (complete closure) or coming very close to each other (partial closure) to block the passage of air-stream. Unlike the consonantal sounds, during the articulation of vowel sounds such as, /I/, /e/, /u/, /ǽ/, etc. no obstruction takes place in the passage of the air-stream. It can be seen in much detail in the chapter phonology.

Now let us look at the ways of describing different consonant and vowel sounds.

5.4.1 Description of Consonant Sounds

Each consonant sound must have certain distinctive features on the basis of which it should be separated from the other sounds. For the sake of finding out the distinctive feature of a consonant sound, that is to describe and classify it, the following parameters can be taken into account.

I. the nature of the air-stream mechanism

II. the state of glottis (voicing)

III. the position of the velum or soft palate (oral/nasal)

IV. the articulators involved (active/passive)

V. the nature of stricture (obstruction of the air-stream)

The nature of air-stream mechanism indicates whether the sound produced is pulmonic, glottalic or velaric on one hand, and egressive or ingressive on the other hand. We have already talked about these air-stream mechanisms in the beginning of this chapter. This may be treated as one of the criteria to distinguish a consonant sound.

The state of glottis indicates whether a sound is voiced (when glottis is closed) or voiceless (when glottis is open). In the case of wide open position of vocal cords, the air-stream passes on smoothly through glottis without causing vibration in the vocal cords and the sounds produced with such a position of vocal cords are called voiceless sounds. The sounds /p/, /t/, /k/, etc. are the voiceless sounds of English language. On the other hand, when vocal cords are loosely drawn together resulting into the narrowing of glottis, the sounds produced in this position cause vibration in vocal cords, and such sounds are called voiced sounds. The sounds /b/, /d/, /g/, etc. of English are the examples of voiced sounds. Thus a sound may be distinguished as voiced or voiceless depending on the position of the glottis.

The position of the velum shows whether a sound is oral (when velum is raised blocking the nasal passage) or nasal (when velum is lowered blocking the oral passage). The raised position of velum produces oral sounds as the air passes through mouth and likewise, its lowered position produces nasal sounds as the air passes through the nose. We have three nasal sounds /m/, /n/ and /ŋ/ in English and all other sounds of English are oral sounds.

During the articulation of a consonant at least two articulators (organs of speech) are involved. These articulators may be classified as active or passive depending on their movement during articulation. That articulator which moves towards another is called active articulator and the other one that remains static is called passive articulator. For example, lower lip and tongue are active articulators which move towards upper lip and the roof of the mouth respectively, whereas the upper lip and the roof of the mouth are considered as passive articulators as they remain passive. On the basis of these articulators, a particular sound may be distinguished.

As regards the strictures involved, it deals with the ways certain obstructions are realized in the passage of air-stream during the articulation of the consonant sounds. These obstructions may occur in the following ways:

I. **Complete closure:** The passage of air-stream is completely blocked for a recognizable moment of time during the articulation of certain consonant sounds. The active and passive articulators come in firm contact to block the passage. This closure may be caused by two lips (in the case of English sounds (/p/

and /b/), tongue and teeth ridge (in the case of English sounds /t/ and /d/), and, back of the tongue and soft palate (in the case of English sounds /k/ and /g/). The English sounds /tʃ/ and /dʒ/ are also produced with this stricture of complete closure.

II. **Partial closure:** During the articulation of English sound /l/, this kind of closure takes place when the air-stream is blocked in the centre of the vocal tract but it escapes through the sides of the tongue.

III. **Intermittent closure:** When tongue, the active articulator strikes against the hard palate, the passive articulator intermittently, the stricture involved is that of intermittent closure. The English sound /r/ in the word 'read' or 'run', etc. is pronounced with this kind of stricture.

IV. **Close approximation:** In a stricture of this kind, the active articulator comes very close to the passive articulator, but the air gets space to pass through causing audible friction. The English sounds /f/, /v/, /z/, etc. are produced with this kind of stricture.

V. **Open approximation:** In the case of this kind of stricture, the active articulator comes near the passive articulator, but the gap between them is wide enough to give sufficient space for air to pass through without causing any friction. The English sounds /w/ and /j/ are produced with this stricture.

Thus, we see that the air-stream is obstructed in different ways to produce a variety of consonant sounds. On the basis of these aforesaid facts, consonant sounds can be satisfactorily described and classified.

Let us now describe some English consonant sounds in the light of the parameters mentioned above.

1. The consonant sound /p/ as pronounced in the word 'pot'

   I. The air-stream used is pulmonic egressive.

   II. It is a voiceless sound as glottis is open.

III. It is an oral sound as velum is raised to block the nasal passage.

IV. Lower lip is active articulator and upper lip is passive articulator.

V. There is stricture of complete closure.

2. The consonant sound /m/ as pronounced in the word 'mat'

I. The air-stream used is pulmonic egressive.

II. It is a voiced sound as glottis is closed.

III. It is a nasal sound as velum is lowered to block the oral passage.

IV. Lower lip is active and upper lip is passive articulator.

V. There is stricture of complete closure.

3. The consonant sound /s/ as pronounced in the word 'speak'

I. The air-stream used is pulmonic egressive.

II. It is a voiceless sound as glottis is open.

III. It is an oral sound as velum is raised to block the nasal passage.

IV. Tongue is active articulator and teeth ridge is passive articulator.

V. There is stricture of close approximation.

5.4.2 Description of Vowel Sounds

As mentioned earlier, the vowel sounds are those during the articulation of which no obstruction takes place in the passage of air-stream, that is to say, the air passes out of oral cavity without causing any friction. Look at the pronunciation of the words: tree, to, true, etc. in which last sounds are vowels during the articulation of which no constriction takes place unlike the initial consonant sounds of these words.

Keeping in view the variety of vowel sounds used in different languages, three criteria have been evolved to describe and classify a vowel sound. These are as follows.

I. the part of the tongue raised towards the roof of the mouth

II. the height up to which the tongue is raised

III. lip rounding

Let us look at each of these one by one.

During the articulation of vowel sounds, tongue is the active articulator, and, hard palate and soft palate are the passive articulators. We can observe it in the articulation of the vowel sounds found in the words like 'reach', 'shirt' and 'zoo'. In the pronunciation of the vowel sound /i:/ represented by the letter 'ea' of 'reach' the front of the tongue is raised towards the hard palate to such a level that no obstruction is caused in the passage of air-stream. In case of /ɜ:/ vowel represented by the letter 'i' of 'shirt' the central part of the tongue is raised towards that part of roof of the mouth which is the adjoining place of the hard palate and soft palate. It rises up to a level that leaves sufficient space for the passage of air without causing friction. Further, in the pronunciation of /u:/ vowel sound represented by the letters 'oo' of 'zoo' the back of the tongue is raised towards soft palate up to a level that does not cause obstruction in the passage of air-stream. Thus, we see that front, central and back parts of the tongue are raised upward during the articulation of vowel sounds. On this basis, the vowel sounds are classified as front, central and back vowels, depending upon the part of the tongue raised. But we have more than one front, central and back vowels as the vowel sound /e/ represented by the letter 'e' of the word 'bed' is also a front vowel, the sound /ə/ represented by letter 'a' of the word 'about' is also a central vowel, and the sound /ɒ/ represented by the letter 'o' of the word 'cot' is also a back vowel. Apart from these vowels, there are some other vowel sounds as well which are front, central and back vowels. In such a condition, it becomes important to evolve the second criterion that is of height up to which the tongue is raised to describe the distinctive qualities of different vowel sounds.

Let us look at the position of the tongue in terms of height it reaches during the articulation of sound /æ/ as represented by the letter 'a' of the word 'bat'. The tongue remains close to lower jaw that shows the open position of the mouth cavity. Again, in the articulation of the vowel sound /i:/ represented by the letter 'ee' of the word 'keep' the tongue is raised up to the maximum height towards the roof of mouth though the air gets sufficient space to escape. This position is considered as close position of the mouth cavity. Thus, in terms of the height, the tongue attains, four reference points have been evolved.

These can be seen through this diagram.

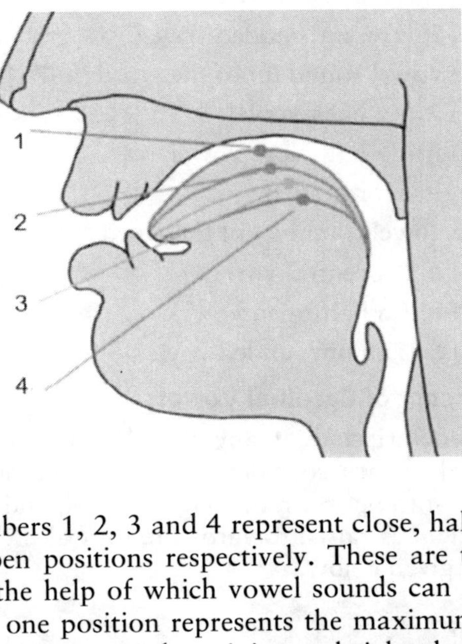

The numbers 1, 2, 3 and 4 represent close, half-close, half-open and open positions respectively. These are the reference points with the help of which vowel sounds can be classified. The number one position represents the maximum height and number four represents the minimum height that the tongue attains during the articulation of some vowels. All these positions have been illustrated in the chapter phonology.

The last criterion of classification of vowel sounds is lip rounding. There are two kinds of vowels: rounded and unrounded based on the rounding of the lips. That is to say, during the articulation of certain vowels, lips are rounded and in some cases it remains normal or unrounded. For example, the vowel sound /e/ represented by the letter 'e' of the word 'fed' is pronounced with unrounded lips, whereas the vowel sound /u/ represented by the letters 'oo' of the word 'book' is pronounced with rounded lips.

Based on these three labels—the portion of the tongue raised, the height attained by the tongue, and the position of the lips, a vowel sound can be described as follows.

1. The vowel sound /i:/ of the word 'teach'
   (a) It is a front vowel.
   (b) It is a close vowel.
   (c) It is an unrounded vowel.
2. The vowel sound /u/ of the word 'full'
   (a) It is a back vowel.
   (b) It is a half-close vowel.
   (c) It is a rounded vowel.
3. The vowel sound /ə/ of the word 'account'
   (a) It is a central vowel.
   (b) It is a half-open vowel.
   (c) It is an unrounded vowel.

5.5 The Concept of Cardinal Vowels

For the description of any vowel sound, eight reference points are taken into consideration. These points are marked on the basis of the portion of tongue raised, and the height up to which tongue is raised towards the roof of the mouth. Look at the figure given below.

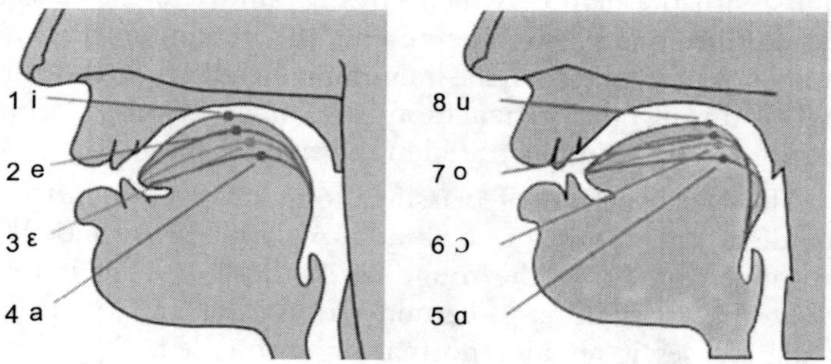

The eight points shown in this figure refer to the whole vowel area. The vowel sounds produced with these eight tongue positions are called cardinal vowels. These are the eight cardinal vowels which represent the reference points as any vowel sound can be described in terms of these points. These eight positions have been named as follows:

Position	Symbol
1. Front close vowel	[i]
2. Front half-close vowel	[e]
3. Front half-open vowel	[ɛ]
4. Front open vowel	[a]
5. Back open vowel	[ɑ]
6. Back half-open vowel	[ɔ]
7. Back half-close vowel	[o]
8. Back close vowel	[u]

From number 1 to 4, the front part of the tongue along with the height it attains has been shown, and from 5 to 8, the back part of the tongue has been shown. The position of height attained has been categorized as close (no. 1), half-close (no. 2), half-open (no. 3), and open (no. 4). These are the imaginary reference points in the light of which any vowel sound can be described.

5.6 The Concept of Diphthongs

Sometimes a pair of vowel sounds is found together in one syllable of a word. Such a pair of vowel sounds is called diphthongs. For example, the word 'hair' has two vowel sounds /e/ and /ə/ that occur in the same syllable as this word is monosyllabic. This /eə/ sound is a diphthong. In the articulation of this diphthong, the tongue position changes from the first vowel /e/ to the second vowel /ə/. There are eight diphthongs in the English language that will be discussed in detail in the chapter phonology.

5.7 The Concept of Triphthongs

Sometimes three vowel sounds occur one after another as part of one syllable in a word. Such a combination of three vowel sounds is called triphthong. The occurrence of three vowel sounds in continuation in the words like 'hour', 'fire', etc. which are pronounced as /a:uə/ and /fa:ɪə/ respectively, are the examples of triphthongs.

5.8 Phonetic Transcription

In many languages of the world, there is a lack of one letter one sound correspondence. For example, in English language which is one of such languages, the letter 'c' represents the sound /k/ in 'cat', /s/ in 'cell' and /ʃ/ in 'social', etc. Likewise, the letters 'ch' represent the sound /k/ in 'chemistry', /tʃ/ in 'chair', /ʃ/ in 'chef', etc. It clearly shows that one letter one sound representation is not there in English language. This spelling-pronunciation incompatibility of languages was one of the factors that induced the linguists to come out with the concept of International Phonetic Alphabet (IPA). This IPA contains one symbol for one sound and it has symbols for the sounds of all the languages of the world. The phonetic transcription is a system of representing the words in the way they are pronounced with the help of phonetic symbols of IPA. In phonetic transcriptions, certain diacritics (symbols) are also used to give accurate picture of the sound produced in the pronunciation of a word. These diacritics mark stress on the syllables, length of a sound, intonation pattern, etc. The knowledge of phonetics helps in making the pronunciation better, especially for non-native learners. With the help of a pronouncing dictionary and phonetic transcription exercises, much improvement in pronunciation can be realized by a non-native learner. It really gives a good idea of sound-letter discrepancy and facilitates the process of learning pronunciation skills.

Let us look at the phonetic transcription of these English words.

School----- /'sku:l/

Glasses---- /'gla:sɪz/

English---- /'ɪŋglɪʃ/

National-- /'næʃnəl/

University- /'ju:nɪ'və:sətɪ/

Exercises

Q1. What is phonetics? What are its branches?

Q2. What do you mean by speech production mechanism? How are the English sounds produced through this mechanism?

Q3. What is the difference between pulmonic egressive and ingressive air-stream?

Q4. Draw a labelled diagram of organs of speech.

Q5. Mention the structure and the function of the vocal cords.

Q6. What is the difference between consonant and vowel sounds?

Q7. How are the consonant sounds described?

Q8. How are the vowel sounds described?

Q9. How many kinds of strictures are involved in the articulation of consonant sounds of English? Describe them with examples.

Q10. What do you mean by cardinal vowels?

Q11. What do you mean by diphthongs?

Q12. Write a note on phonetic transcription.

Q13. Write short notes on the differences between the following.

I. Front and back vowels

II. Voiced and voiceless sounds

III. Oral and nasal sounds

IV. Active and passive articulators

Q14. Phonetically transcribe the following words.

Market	Psychology
Animal	Chauvinism
Language	Through
Medicine	Rough
Bachelor	Planning
Socialize	Intelligent

Q15. Make a separate list of diphthongs from the following words. Take help of dictionary if required.

Boy	Cow	Near
Oil	Air	Play
Late	High	Paint
Poor	Go	Tour

Phonology of English

6

6.1 Phonetics and Phonology

As we have seen that phonetics is the study of human speech sounds in general, phonology is the study of speech sounds of a particular language. That is to say, when we study the sounds of a language, it is phonological study. While phonetics talks about the general properties of speech sounds such as, their production, transmission and reception along with the ways of their description, phonology talks about the organization of sounds in a particular language.

Phonetics takes into account the total number of human speech sounds used in different languages of the world, whereas phonology deals with what number of these sounds is used in a particular language such as, English, Arabic, etc. On this basis, it can be said that the former is all inclusive, while the latter is exclusive.

In this chapter, we will talk about the phonology of English language. How many sounds are used in English language, how these sounds are combined (organized) in the form of words, how they are produced and described, all such matters are discussed in phonology. We see that the word 'pin' is a combination of /p/, /ɪ/ and /n/ sounds. It represents a consonant-vowel-consonant combination. This pattern of consonant and vowel sounds is looked into minutely to establish the nature of the English phonological system. Apart from this, the supra-segmental features like stress, rhythm and intonation patterns are also taken into account in phonology. Thus, phonology studies all aspects of sounds of a language very comprehensively.

6.2 Description of English Sounds

There are forty-four sounds in English (R.P.) language. Out of these, twenty-four sounds are consonants, and twenty sounds are vowels. Among these vowels, twelve sounds are pure vowels or monophthongs and eight sounds are diphthongs. Let us look at all these sounds one by one.

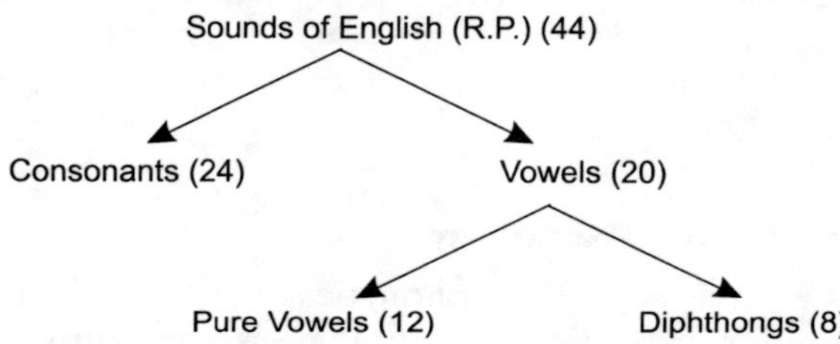

6.2.1 English Consonants

All the twenty–four consonants of English language can be described in terms of three labels—place of articulation, manner of articulation and voicing pattern as we have seen in the chapter "Phonetics". Each consonant sound shows distinction from one another in at least one of these three characteristics, and thus, it is identified on this basis. For example, the sounds /p/ and /b/ are the same in place of articulation (bilabial), and manner of articulation (plosive), but they differ in voicing pattern as former is voiceless while latter is voiced. On this basis, these two sounds are distinguished. Therefore only three labels have been considered to establish the identity of each consonant sound. Let us look at this chart of English consonants which shows three labels for each sound.

This chart shows the kinds of consonant sounds found in English language. The classification of these sounds according to manner of articulation indicates the nature of stricture (blockage of air-stream) involved, that is, how the passage of air-stream is blocked during the articulation. On the other hand, place of articulation indicates the active and passive articulators' role, that is, the organs of speech involved in articulation. The voicing shows the position of vocal cords. The closed position of vocal cords produces voiced sounds, and

Consonants of English (R.P.)

Place of articulation	Manner of Articulation											
	Plosive		Affricate		Nasal		Fricative		Lateral		Approximants	
	vl	vd	vl	vd	vl	vd	vl	vd	vl	vd	vl	vd
Bilabial	p	b				m						w
Labio-dental							f	v				
Dental							θ	ð				
Alveolar	t	d				n	s	z		l		
Post-alveolar												r
Palato-alveolar			tʃ	dʒ			ʃ	ʒ				
Palatal												j
Velar	k	g				ŋ						
Glottal							h					
vl– voiceless vd - voiced												

the open position produces voiceless sounds. Because of the closed position, vibration takes place in vocal cords during articulation and it results into voiced sounds, whereas its open position does not cause vibration, and so, the sounds produced are voiceless. Out of these three labels, manner of articulation is the most technical, and so, it is better to describe these sounds under this type. The chart shows that the English language has the following types of consonant sounds.

I. Plosives— /p/, /b/, /t/, /d/, /k/, /g/

II. Affricates— /tʃ/, /dʒ/

III. Nasals— /m/, /n/, /ŋ/

IV. Fricatives— /f/, /v/, /θ/, /ð/, /s/, /z/, /ʃ/, /ʒ/, /h/

V. Laterals— /l/

VI. Approximants— /w/, /r/, /j/

Let us describe these sounds one by one.

I. Plosives

These sounds are produced with a stricture of complete closure and sudden release of air causing a kind of explosive effect. Because of the complete closure of air-passage, these sounds are called stop sounds also. Soft palate is raised to block the nasal passage and so these are oral sounds.

During the articulation of the sounds /p/ and /b/, complete closure is caused by the two lips, therefore, these are bilabial sounds (place of articulation). The two lips block the passage of air for a recognizable moment and then sudden release takes place. Likewise, during the articulation of /t/ and /d/, complete closure is caused by the tip of the tongue and alveolar ridge, and so these sounds are alveolar sounds (place of articulation). The sounds /k/ and /g/ are produced by the complete closure caused by the back of the tongue and soft palate (velum), and so these sounds are velar (place of articulation). Out of these six plosives, /p/, /t/ and /k/ are voiceless, and /b/, /d/ and /g/ are voiced, depending on the vibration of vocal cords during their articulation.

II. Affricates

These sounds are also produced with the stricture of complete closure, but here the release of air is comparatively slow that causes an audible friction. The release is slow because the articulators gradually move apart, not suddenly like plosives. Soft palate is raised to block the nasal passage.

The sounds /tʃ/ and /dʒ/ are affricates. During the articulation of these sounds the complete closure is caused by the tip of the tongue and alveolar ridge, but front of the tongue is also raised towards the hard palate making these sounds palato-alveolar (place of articulation). /tʃ/ is a voiceless sound and /dʒ/ is a voiced sound depending on the vibration of the vocal cords during their articulation.

III. Nasals

These sounds are produced with the stricture of complete oral closure and release of air through the nose. Since the air is released through nasal passage, the sounds are called nasal.

/m/, /n/ and /ŋ/ are the three nasal sounds in English. During the articulation of /m/, the complete oral closure is caused by the two lips, and so, it is a bilabial sound (place of articulation). In the articulation of /n/ sound, the complete oral closure is caused by the tip of the tongue and alveolar ridge, and so, it is an alveolar sound (place of articulation). In the articulation of /ŋ/ sound, the complete oral closure is caused by the back of the tongue and the soft palate (velum), and so, it is a velar sound (place of articulation). All these nasal sounds are voiced sounds as vocal cords vibrate during their articulation.

IV. Fricatives

These sounds are produced with a stricture of close approximation that means the two organs come very close to each other but some space is left between them through which the air escapes causing audible friction. Nasal passage is blocked by the raised soft palate. During the articulation of the sounds /f/ and /v/, this kind of approximate closure is caused by the lower lip and the upper teeth, and so, these sounds are called labio-dental (place of articulation).

In the articulation of the sounds /θ/ and /ð/, the closure is caused by the tip of the tongue and the upper teeth, and so, these sounds are called dental (place of articulation). Further, in the articulation of /s/ and /z/, the closure is caused by the tip of the tongue and the alveolar ridge, and so, these sounds are called alveolar (place of articulation).

Again, in the articulation of /ʃ/, /ʒ/, the closure is caused by the tip of the tongue and the alveolar ridge, but the front of the tongue is also raised towards the hard palate, and so, these sounds are called palato-alveolar sounds (place of articulation). The last fricative sound is /h/ which is articulated with the narrowing of the glottis, and so, it is called glottal (place of articulation). Out of these nine fricative sounds, /f/, /θ/, /s/, /ʃ/ and /h/ are voiceless, and the rest are the voiced sounds depending on the vibration of the vocal cords during their articulation.

V. Lateral

These sounds are produced with a stricture of complete closure in the centre of the vocal tract, but air escapes through the sides of the tongue. Nasal passage is blocked by the raised soft palate. During the articulation of /l/ sound, the closure is caused by the tip or blade of the tongue and the alveolar ridge, and so, this sound is alveolar (place of articulation). It is a voiced sound because the vocal cords vibrate during its articulation.

VI. Approximants

These are the sounds produced with a stricture of open approximation. That means during the articulation of these sounds, the gap between the active and passive articulators is wide enough through which the air escapes without any friction. Nasal passage is closed by the raised soft palate. The sound /r/ is articulated with the raising of the tip of the tongue towards the back of the alveolar ridge. Therefore, this sound is post-alveolar (place of articulation). Here, the space between the tip of the tongue and alveolar ridge is quite sufficient for the frictionless continuant.

The sound /w/ is articulated with the rounding of the lips like vowel sounds. Therefore, this sound is called semi-vowel also. Since both the lips are articulators, this sound is bilabial (place of articulation). The sound /j/ is articulated with the tongue position like vowel sounds where sufficient space is left for the passage of air stream without coming across any constriction. Here the front of the tongue is raised towards the entire palatal region, and so, this sound is palatal (place of articulation). This sound is also called semi-vowel because of its similarity with vowel sounds in terms of articulation. All of these approximants are voiced sounds as vocal cords vibrate during their articulation.

6.2.2 English Vowels

All the vowels used in English have been classified as monophthongs (pure vowels) and diphthongs. These monophthongs are single vowels, and so, they are called pure vowels also. Diphthongs are double vowels found in one syllable as we have already seen earlier. There are twelve pure vowels and eight diphthongs in English language that can be seen as follows.

Pure Vowels

Symbol	Example	Transcription	
i:-	as found in the word – reach	/ri:tʃ/	
I-	as found in the word – rich	/rItʃ/	
e-	as found in the word – bed	/bed/	Front vowels
æ-	as found in the word – bat	/bæt/	
ə:-	as found in the word – shirt	/ʃə:t/	
ə-	as found in the word – about	/əbaUt/	Central vowels
Λ-	as found in the word – cup	/kΛp/	
u:-	as found in the word – fruit	/fru:t/	
U-	as found in the word – book	/bUk/	
Ɔ:-	as found in the word – fought	/fƆ:t/	Back vowels
ɒ-	as found in the word – pot	/pɒt/	
a:-	as found in the word – car	/ka:/	

Diphthongs

eI - as found in the word – make /meIk/
ƆI- as found in the word – toy /tƆI/
aI- as found in the word – cry /kraI/
Iə- as found in the word – near /nIə/
eə- as found in the word – hair /heə/
Uə- as found in the word – poor /pUə/
əU- as found in the word – so /səU/
aU- as found in the word – cow /caU/

All of these symbols used for vowel sounds have been taken from A.C. Gimson's "An Introduction to Pronunciation of English". As these symbols are commonly used in the books of phonetics, *English Phonology* and *Oxford Dictionary*, it will be convenient for the readers to understand them here.

As we have already talked at length about the ways of description of vowel sounds in the chapter phonetics, here we will describe these English vowels in that frame, i.e. in terms of the following.

(a) the part of the tongue raised towards the roof of the mouth

(b) the height up to which the tongue is raised

(c) the lip rounding

Now look at the diagram below that shows the position of the tongue during the articulation of the English vowels.

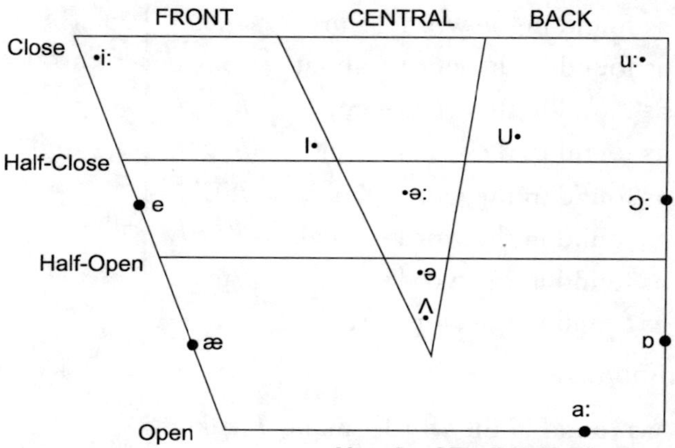

Vowels of English (R.P.)

Let us describe these pure vowels one by one.

Front Vowels

(I) /i:/ This vowel sound is produced when the front of the tongue is raised towards the hard palate up to the height of the close position. This close position is an imaginary level of height as described earlier up to which the front part of the tongue is raised. Even above this position, there is sufficient space between the tongue and hard palate through which air escapes easily. This vowel is thus described as front (because front part of the tongue is raised), close (because the tongue is raised up to close position), and unrounded (because the lips are spread not round). It can be seen in the words teach, speech, etc.

(II) /I/ In the articulation of this vowel, the back part of the front of the tongue is raised towards the hard palate up to a point just above the half-close position. The lips are spread. Therefore, this vowel is described as front unrounded vowel above the half-close position. It can be seen in the words bit, pit, etc.

(III) /e/ In the articulation of this vowel, the front of the tongue is raised towards the hard palate up to a point between half-close and half-open positions. The lips are spread. Therefore, this vowel is described as front unrounded vowel between the half-close and the half-open positions. It can be seen in the words bed, said, etc.

(IV) /æ/ In the articulation of this vowel, the front of the tongue is raised towards the hard palate to a point above the open position. The lips are spread. Therefore, this vowel is described as front unrounded vowel above the open position. It can be seen in the words pat, mat, etc.

Central Vowels

(I) /ə:/ In the articulation of this vowel, the central part (between the front and the back) of the tongue is raised towards the adjoining part of soft palate and hard palate to a point between half-open and half-close positions. The lips are spread. Therefore, this vowel is described as central unrounded vowel between half-open and half-close positions. It can be seen in the words bird, shirt, etc.

(II) /ə/ In the articulation of this vowel, the central part of the tongue is raised towards the adjoining part of the hard palate and soft palate to a point below the half-open position. The lips are spread. Therefore, this vowel is described as central unrounded vowel below the half-open position. It can be seen in the words about, around, etc.

(III) /Λ/ In the articulation of this vowel, the central part of the tongue is raised towards the adjoining part of the hard palate and soft palate above the open position. The lips are spread. Therefore, this vowel is described as central unrounded vowel above the open position. It can be seen in the words cup, but, shut, etc.

Back Vowels

(I) /u:/ In the articulation of this vowel, the back of the tongue is raised towards the soft palate to a point near the close position. The lips are rounded. Therefore, this vowel is described as back close rounded vowel. It can be seen in the words food, two, etc.

(II) /U/ In the articulation of this vowel, the back of the tongue is raised towards the soft palate to a point above the half-close position. The lips are rounded. Therefore, this vowel is described as a back rounded vowel above the half-close position. It can be seen in the words book, full, etc.

(III) /Ɔ:/ In the articulation of this vowel, the back of the tongue is raised towards the soft palate to a point between half-close and half-open positions. The lips are rounded. Therefore, this vowel is described as a back rounded vowel between the half-close and the half-open positions. It can be seen in the words fought, horse, etc.

(IV) /ɒ/ In the articulation of this vowel, the back of the tongue is raised towards the soft palate to a point between the open and half-open positions. The lips are rounded. Therefore, this vowel is described as back rounded vowel between the open and half-open positions. It can be seen in the words like pot, cot, etc.

(V) /a:/ In the articulation of this vowel, the back of the tongue is raised towards the soft palate up to the open position. The lips are spread. Therefore this vowel is described as back open unrounded vowel. It can be seen in the words mar, war, etc.

Out of these twelve pure vowels, /i:/, / ə:/, /u:/, /Ɔ:/, and /a:/ are long vowels and /I/, /e/, /æ/, /Λ/, /ə/, /ɒ/ and /U/ are short vowels. The diacritic [:] indicates the length. These long vowels are pronounced for a comparatively long time. Apart from this, it is a convention that when a vowel is followed by a voiced sound, it is elongated, and when it is followed by a voiceless sound, it is shortened. That is to say, /i:/ in the word 'bead' is longer than it is in the word 'beat'. Likewise, the vowel /I/ in the word 'bid' is longer than it is in the word 'bit'.

Diphthongs

We have talked that diphthongs are vowel glides, i.e. during the articulation of a diphthong a glide from one vowel to another vowel takes place. Usually the first vowel of a diphthong is longer and louder than the second. Let us describe each of these diphthongs presented in the figures 1 and 2. The direction of the arrow indicates the movement from one vowel to another. The diagram clearly shows that three diphthongs end with /I/ (eI, aI, ƆI), another three diphthongs end with /ə/ (Iə, Uə, eə) and the rest two diphthongs end with /U/ (aU, əU).

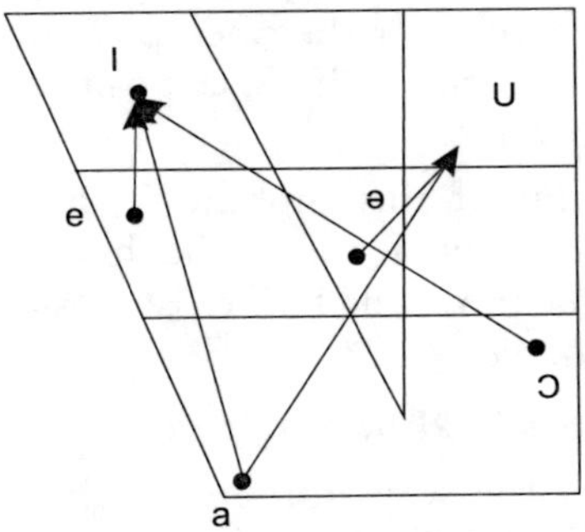

Fig. 1 (eI, ƆI, aU, əU, aI)

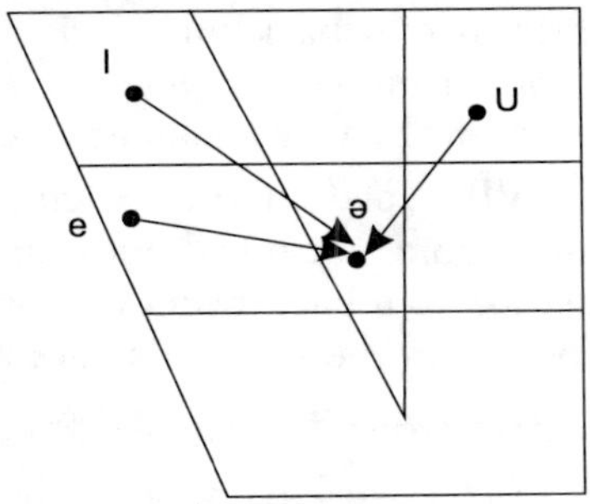

Fig. 2 (eə, Iə, Uə)

(I) /eI/ In the articulation of this diphthong, a glide starts from the front unrounded vowel between half-open and half-close position to a front unrounded vowel just above the half-close position. It occurs in the words paint, make, etc.

(II) /aI/ In the articulation of this diphthong, a glide starts from a centralized front open unrounded vowel to a front unrounded vowel just above half-close position. It occurs in the words try, fly, etc.

(III) /ƆI/ In the articulation of this diphthong, a glide takes place from a back rounded vowel between open and half-open position to a front unrounded vowel just above half-close position. It occurs in words toy, ploy, etc.

(IV) /Iə/ In the articulation of this diphthong, a glide takes place from a front unrounded vowel just above the half-close position to a central unrounded vowel just below the half-open position. It occurs in the words like near, fear, etc.

(V) /Uə/ In the articulation of this diphthong, a glide takes place from a back rounded vowel just above the half-close position to a central unrounded vowel just below the half-open position. It occurs in the words like poor, tour, etc.

(VI) /eə/ In the articulation of this diphthong, a glide starts from a front unrounded vowel between half-open and half-close position to a central unrounded vowel just below the half open position. It occurs in the words like pair, share, etc.

(VII) /aU/ In the articulation of this diphthong, a glide starts from a back unrounded vowel near the open position to a back rounded vowel just above the half-close position. It occurs in the words like now, cow, etc.

(VIII) /əU/ In the articulation of this diphthong, a glide starts from a central unrounded vowel above the half-open position to a back rounded vowel above the half-close position. It occurs in the words like go, no, etc.

6.3 Some Fundamental Concepts in Phonology

So far we have talked about the ways different sounds of English language are produced and distinguished from one another. The next aspect of phonology is concerned with how these sounds are grouped to produce meaningful words. A sensible look at English words makes it clear that usually a consonant and a vowel sound combination works as the fundamental unit in words. Take for example the words like—pen, toy, keep, city, famous, school, etc. in all of these, the combination of consonant and vowel is clearly visible that constitutes a syllable. Apart from this, there are certain other phonological characteristics as well that need to be analyzed for a proper understanding of underlying pattern of sounds in English language. It is seen that a particular sound occurs in different forms in different words, i.e. a kind of variation is realized in the articulation of some sounds in certain specific positions in words. A plosive sound is not plosive in all the positions. Likewise a nasal sound becomes dental in certain words. To understand such characteristics of sounds certain terminologies have been evolved for concept formation. Let us have a look at these terminologies.

6.3.1 Phoneme

A phoneme is the minimal distinct sound of a language. That is to say, out of all the possible sounds (consonants and vowels) produced by the organs of speech, whatever sounds are used in a particular language, these are usually considered as phonemes. In English language, there are forty-four phonemes depending on the number of distinctive sounds used in it. A phoneme is called minimal or smallest because it cannot be further divided, and it is distinct because the replacement of one phoneme by another changes a word. Look at the words—kit and sit. These words are different because of their initial sounds only. Therefore, these sounds /k/ and /s/ are recognized as distinct phonemes. Likewise, the words—bit and bat are different because of difference in the middle vowel sounds. Hence these /I/ and /æ/ sounds are separate phonemes, as a word changes after their inclusion or exclusion in it. A phoneme is kept under slant lines, as the phonemes given above indicate.

6.3.2 Allophone

Sometimes a phoneme is phonetically realized in different ways in different words. For example, the phoneme /l/ is pronounced in the word 'lock' more prominently than it is pronounced in the word 'bottle'. In the former it is very clear, whereas in the latter it is not clear (dark). Phonetically, we have two realizations of /l/ that is clear and dark. These two varieties of the phoneme /l/ are considered as allophones. Likewise, we have two varieties of /p/, /t/ and /k/ phonemes—the aspirated and unaspirated. The aspirated forms are realized as /p^h/, /t^h/, and /k^h/ in the words where these sounds occur in initial positions in stressed syllables. We can find these aspirated forms in the words like problem, ticket, captain, where the first syllables are stressed and hence these sounds are realized as /p^h/, /t^h/ and /k^h/. These phonemes are unaspirated in the words like speech, stock, skin, as they do not occur in initial positions, and so, they are realized as /p/, /t/ and /k/. Hence, these aspirated and unaspirated varieties are the allophones.

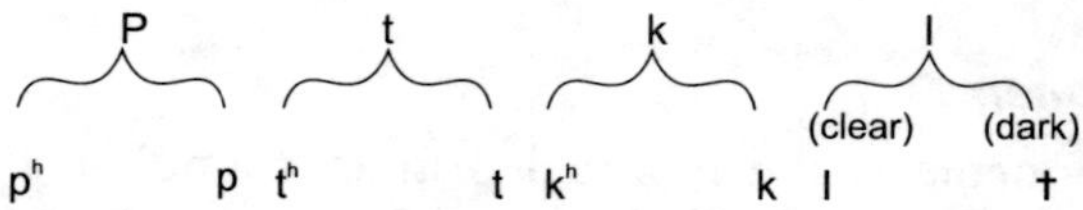

Here it can be said that the concept of phoneme is an abstract concept and its actual realization takes place in the form of allophones. Therefore, these allophones are the variants (the alternative realizations) of phonemes.

6.3.3 Minimal Pair

A minimal pair is that pair of words which has only one sound different between the two words. For example—the words *tip* and *lip* are the minimal pair as there is difference in initial sounds /t/ and /l/ only. This concept of minimal pair is useful in understanding many other phonological concepts.

6.3.4 Phonotactics

It deals with that aspect of phonology which talks about the permissible constituents of a syllable in a language. It is seen that in English, a consonant-vowel-consonant combination is very common as we have words like—big, sit, cat, etc. which conform to this pattern. In the constitution of a syllable and subsequently a word, only a certain set of phonemes is used. To clarify it further, a combination of five or more consonants in continuation is not permissible in English. The consonantal clusters like 'mks' 'rlt' 'qmps', etc. do not occur in English, whereas the consonantal clusters like 'str' (strange), 'lfth' (twelfth), 'tr' (train), etc. are found. Such a phonological phenomenon is language specific as we can find unacceptable consonantal clusters of English, acceptable in any other language. Thus, phonotactics takes into account the phonological constraints that limit the permissible combination of phonemes in syllables of a language.

6.3.5 Phonetic Environment

By the term phonetic environment of a phoneme, we mean the sound that precedes it and the sound that follows it. For example, the phonetic environment of the phoneme /p/ in the word 'speak' is—sound /s/ precedes it and sound /i:/ follows it.

That is to say, phonetic environment decides the boundary of a phoneme.

6.3.6 Syllable

A syllable is a larger sound unit than a phoneme in a word. It consists of one or more than one phoneme. It is usually that combination of sounds which is produced as a result of one chest pulse, as we know that a word is articulated with several muscular movements (chest pulses) depending on the number of consonant and vowel sounds in it. A syllable has usually a vowel sound as an essential element along with consonant sounds. We have syllables of only vowel sound also, such as 'a', 'I', etc. On the other hand, we have syllables without vowel sounds also, such as the second syllable of the words button, little, etc. In English language, there are words of one syllable like pat (monosyllabic), two syllables like problem (disyllabic), three syllables like potato (trisyllabic), etc. We can realize the number of chest pulses during the articulation of these words. Each chest pulse produces one syllable. A vowel sound generally occupies the central place in a syllable. A reinforced chest pulse produces a stressed syllable as we have stressed and unstressed syllable sequences in English words.

6.3.7 Aspiration

All the voiceless plosives /p/, /t/ and /k/ of English language are pronounced with additional /h/ sound when they occur in initial position in a stressed syllable. This change of /p/, /t/ and /k/ into /p^h/, /t^h/ and /k^h/ is called aspiration. For example, the word 'pin' is realized as /p^hIn/, 'talk' as /t^hƆ:k/ and 'calm' as /k^ha:m/ as these are all monosyllabic words and so when stressed, these plosives get aspirated.

6.4 Phonemic Analysis

A phoneme is a language specific entity, that is to say, different languages have different sets of phonemes. To clarify it further, a phoneme of English language may or may not be found in other languages. For example, the phoneme /p/ of English language does not exist in Arabic, and likewise the Arabic phoneme /ţ/ is not found in English. The concept of phonemic analysis, therefore, deals with certain principles that help us in identification of phonemes belonging to a particular language. Let us look at some of these principles.

6.4.1 The Principle of Contrastive Distribution

When two sounds of a language are found in the same phonetic environment and replacement of one by the other changes the meaning of words, then these two sounds are two separate phonemes of that language. Consider the two words—pat and mat, which are the minimal pairs. The phonetic environment for the sounds /p/ and /m/ are the same here as they are not preceded by any sound and followed by the same vowel /æ/. The replacement of one by the other changes the meaning of the words. It means that these two sounds are in contrastive distribution and hence they are two distinct phonemes of English language, as these words are of English language. To make it clear further, this principle of contrastive distribution establishes that two sounds will be separate phonemes only when—

(a) they occur in the same phonetic environment, and

(b) their replacement by each other alters the meaning of the words.

6.4.2 The Principle of Complementary Distribution

When two sounds used in a language do not occur in the same phonetic environment and the replacement of one by the other does not change the meaning of a word, then these two sounds are considered to be in complementary distribution. Consider the words 'peak' and 'speak'. The sounds represented by the letter /p/ in both the words are different. In peak, it is aspirated and realized as /p^h/, and in speak, it is unaspirated and realized as /p/. The phonetic environment of these sounds is different and the replacement of one by the other does not change the meaning of the words. That is to say, if /p^h/ of peak is changed into /p/, its meaning will not change. Likewise, if /p/ unaspirated sound of 'speak' is changed into aspirated /p^h/, the meaning of the word speak will remain the same. It means that these two sounds are in complementary distribution, and so, they are not the separate phonemes. They are all allophones of English language. Thus, the principle of complementary distribution establishes that two sounds will be allophones only when—

(a) they occur in different phonetic environment, and

(b) their replacement by each other does not change the meaning of the words.

6.4.3 The Principle of Free Variation

When two sounds used in a language occur in the same phonetic environment and the replacement of one by the other does not change the meaning of words, then these two sounds are considered to be in free variation. Consider the final sounds of the words—stop and flop. These sounds are different in the sense that in one word, it may be exploded or vice versa, depending on the choice of the speaker, as we know that plosive sounds usually lose explosion in words in final positions. But at the same time, they can be articulated with explosion as well. Here, these sounds occur in the same phonetic environment and their replacement by each other will not change the meaning of words. Hence, they are the sounds in free variation. The sounds that occur in free variation can be pronounced in both the ways as we pronounce the initial sounds of the word 'either' as /aɪ/ or /i:/. To sum up, the principle of free variation establishes that two sounds will be in free variation if—

(a) they occur in the same phonetic environment, and

(b) their replacement by each other does not change the meaning of the words.

These principles of phonemic analysis help us in proper understanding of the characteristics of sounds of a language. On the basis of these principles, we can distinguish different varieties of sounds such as, phonemes, allophones and free variants.

6.5 Phonemic Transcription

It is a method of presenting all the sounds used in pronunciation of a word in the form of phonemes. Unlike phonetic transcription, only phonemes are used here to represent the sounds without the stress mark or length of sounds, etc. Phonemic transcription is called broad transcription, as we do not represent all the features of speech sounds here like phonetic one that is narrow transcription. Look at the phonemic transcription of these words.

Examination	/IgzæmIneIʃn/
Advertisement	/ədvə:tIzmənt/
Popularity	/pɒpjUlærətI/
Method	/meɵəd/

Thus, it is clear that only the symbols of phonemes are used to represent the sounds of the words in phonemic transcription. In the initial stages of learning pronunciation, these phonemic transcription exercises are very beneficial.

6.6 Prosodic or Supra-segmental Features

Till now we have talked much about each distinct sound of English language that is realized in various forms in different words. Each of these sounds is considered as distinct segments (phonemes), the smallest units of speech. Now we shall talk about the bigger units of speech along with some distinctive phonological features of English language realized in connected speeches or long utterances. Since these features are associated with the units larger than that of segments, we call them prosodic or supra-segmental features. Under this heading we shall talk about stress, rhythm and intonation.

6.6.1 Stress

We have seen earlier that a syllable is a group of phonemes. The words of English are made up of one or more than one syllable depending on the length of a word. Each syllable is a product of one chest pulse or breath force. When a particular syllable is produced with a strong breath force, it is considered to be stressed. Thus, stress is that characteristic of sound which is realized when a particular syllable is articulated with a strong breath force. Usually the content words that give the main idea of a sentence are stressed, whereas the function/structure words which are required to perform grammatical function in a sentence are not stressed. Content words are generally nouns, adjectives and main verbs, whereas function words are articles, pronouns, prepositions, auxiliaries, conjunctions, etc. In English language, these stressed syllables occur at regular intervals in words and connected speeches. Because of this feature, English is considered as a stress-timed language unlike Hindi a syllable-timed language where each syllable is articulated with equal force and in equal span of time. A stressed syllable is marked with a small vertical bar above it. Look at some examples.

Past	- Monosyllabic	/'p^{h}a:st/
City	- Disyllabic	/'sItI/
Potato	- Trisyllabic	/pə't^{h}eItəU/
Information	- Tetrasyllabic	/ˌInfə'meIʃn/
Communication	- Pentasyllabic	/kəˌmju:nɪ'keIʃn/

Thus, we see that one syllable is stressed in each word as it is pronounced with strong breath force. In multi-syllabic words, even more than one syllable is stressed but not with equal force. The most prominent syllables bear the primary stress (shown by vertical bars above), and less prominent syllables bear the secondary stress (shown by vertical bars below). Unstressed syllables remain unmarked.

6.6.2 Rhythm

Rhythm is a musical quality of speech that intends to create a soothing impression on the mind of the listeners. In order to realize this effect in a language, certain methods are evolved. The English language is marked with this rhythmic quality which is realized when we take into account the certain technicalities involved in it. We saw that content words are stressed and function words are unstressed in connected speech. Content words are stressed to make the meaning of a sentence very clear. Look at this sentence.

'Players have 'gone to 'Delhi.

Here, all the content words are stressed, marked with vertical bars, and structure/function words—'have' and 'to' are not stressed. These stressed and unstressed syllables together constitute rhythm units. Now let us divide the stressed and unstressed syllables into such units which are also called foot.

'Players have/ 'gone to/ 'Delhi.

rhythm units
(stress groups)

As English is a stress-timed language, during the articulation of each of these units, almost equal time should be taken by a speaker. This characteristic of English language gives it rhythm. The concept of rhythm is associated with time factor. Each of these feet is called rhythm unit or stress group. A rhythm unit is, thus, made up of one stressed syllable and all unstressed syllables that go with it. On this basis, it can be said that rhythm is that phonological feature of English language which is realized in connected speech when sentences are articulated with proper stress on required syllables along with the consideration of equal time span in articulation for each stress group.

6.6.3 Intonation

During the production of speech sounds, the vibration of vocal cords is a common phenomenon. The degree of vibration depends on the frequency with which vocal cords open and close per second. This relationship between frequency and vibration is directly proportional, i.e. more frequency results into more vibration. In continuous speech this frequency always keeps on changing. The rate of change of this frequency is called pitch. This change of pitch results into rise and fall of voice in continuous speech that is called intonation. When the pitch movement is from low to high, it causes rising tone. When the pitch movement is from high to low, it causes falling tone. In some cases, it falls first and then rises, and vice versa producing a falling-rising and rising-falling tone respectively.

Look at these sentences.

My father is a ˋteacher. (falling tone)

Are you ˏgoing? (rising tone)

I come here ˇsometimes. (falling-rising tone)

Is he ˆsure it will work? (rising-falling tone)

The mark [ˋ] indicates falling tone, the mark [ˊ] indicates rising tone, the mark [ˇ] indicates falling-rising tone and the mark [ˆ] indicates rising-falling tone. In these sentences, the pitch movement takes place on the words *teacher, going, sometimes,* and *sure* as shown through the marks along with the nature of tone indicated in the brackets. Here it is important to note that pitch change takes place on stressed syllables depending on the meaning the speaker wants to convey in an utterance. For instance, in the first sentence the speaker wants to convey that his father is nothing else but a teacher, and so, pitch change occurs on the first syllable of the word *teacher*. Such is the case with other three sentences given above where the pitch changes on the stressed syllables of the words that the speaker wants to highlight. The syllable on which the pitch change occurs is called tonic syllable. Thus, a tonic syllable is decided by a speaker on the basis of what he/she wants to highlight in an utterance. The stressed syllables on which no pitch movement occurs are said to be on level tones (static). The level tones are indicated by usual stress marks used for primary (high voice) and secondary (low voice) stresses. In the case of continuous or long utterances, we take pauses in between to breath. Therefore, long utterances are divided into small groups on the basis of pauses. Such small groups of utterances are called tone/breath/sense groups. An utterance may be of one tone group as is the case with all the sentences above, and in each tone group there may be level tones with a tonic syllable as an essential constituent. In complex sentences like—'When I was in office, he came to me as he needed my advice'. The three clauses of this sentence constitute the three tone groups as each of the tone group requires a pause for natural articulation.

Intonation as a phonological feature is used to serve some important functions in utterances. It helps in making the meaning of utterances clear by showing the emphasis of the speakers on specific words having tonic syllables. It largely indicates the mood and attitude of the speakers, as a rising tone in wh-question usually shows the friendly gesture. It performs grammatical functions also. For instance, a statement with rising tone changes a declarative sentence into interrogative. Look at these sentences.

My friend is a ˋteacher. (declarative)

My friend is a ˏteacher. (interrogative)

Here, the first sentence is declarative simply because there is falling tone on the word 'teacher'. The second sentence becomes interrogative due to the rising tone on the same word, where the speaker wants to be sure whether his friend is a teacher. Thus, intonation plays a very important role in English sentences.

6.7 Some Distinct Features of Connected Speech

The whole act of verbal communication operates successfully with the putting together of phonemes, the smallest distinct items, into bigger units like syllables, words, and sentences. We have seen that in English language forty-four phonemes are used and they are realized in allophonic forms in different phonetic environments increasing further this number of distinctly identifiable sounds. It so happens because the quality of sounds undergoes certain phonological changes or in some cases even some sounds are lost when used in different combinations in the speech act. These changes have led to the emergence of some linguistic concepts like Assimilation, Elision, Juncture, etc. For the sake of proper understanding of all these phenomena, it is important to be aware of these terms.

6.7.1 Assimilation

In continuous speech, some sounds lose their original quality in terms of any of these variables like place of articulation, manner of articulation, and voicing, under the influence of preceding or following sound. This process of change in quality of a sound under the influence of another sound is called assimilation. We can understand it better with the help of some examples. The sound /n/ in the word *tenth* changes from alveolar to dental under the influence of the following sound /θ/ that is dental. Likewise, the sound /m/ that is originally a bilabial sound changes into a labio-dental sound in the word *comfort* under the influence of /f/ sound that is labio-dental. In both of these examples, we find that the following sounds /θ/ and /f/, change the preceding sounds /n/ and /m/ respectively. Such assimilations are called regressive where a preceding sound acquires the feature of a succeeding sound. On the other hand, some preceding sounds change the feature of succeeding sounds, as for example, the sound /p/ in the word *play* changes the sound /l/ from voiced into voiceless under its influence. Such assimilations are called progressive.

This assimilation takes place within a word as well as between the words. All the examples given above, show assimilation within the words. Let us pronounce the words *in the taxi,* where we find that /n/ sound of 'in' changes into a dental sound under the influence of the initial /ð/ sound of the word *the*. Likewise, in the group of words *came from,* /m/ sound of 'came' changes from a bilabial sound into a labio-dental sound under the effect of /f/ sound of the word *from*. So far, we have seen the cases of assimilation in consonant sounds only, but vowels also undergo such changes. For instance, all the vowels preceded and followed by nasal sounds, especially in monosyllabic words like *man, bomb, noun, mom*, etc. become nasalized sounds under the influence of nasal sounds that follow them. Thus, assimilation as a phonological phenomenon is widely realized in connected speech and its awareness helps us sound natural in our speech.

6.7.2 Elision

Elision is that phonological phenomenon in which certain sounds are lost or get elided when they occur in a particular kind of phonetic environment in connected speech. It usually happens in the case of two similar sounds occurring one after another. For instance, in the articulation of the groups of words like 'last time' 'fast track' 'right turn', we find that /t/ sound of the first words gets lost when articulated in continuation. These groups of words are realized as /la:s taIm/, /fa:s træk/, /raI tə:n/ respectively, in actual pronunciation. The cases of elision are found within the words also. In the words like *tonight,* pronounced as /tənaIt/, and *police*, pronounced as

/pəli:s/, /ə/ sound gets dropped, making /tn/ and /pl/ syllabic consonants when they occur in connected speech. Moreover, negatives attached to auxiliaries like haven't, don't, etc. represent the examples of elision. Elision indicates the pace of fast moving highly mechanical world where economy and precision stand as the guiding force. The awareness of elision as a concept helps in understanding native speakers to a large extent.

6.7.3 Juncture

Juncture is that concept related to continuous speech in which the lack of recognizable pause between two words or syllables results into the complete difference in meaning of the expressions. Look at these groups of words.

I scream	(ice cream)
A name	(an aim)
That stuff	(that's tough)
In appropriate situations	(inappropriate situations)

When these expressions are uttered without giving the required degree of pause between them, there is immense possibility of loss of communication. The expressions given in the brackets may replace the intended expressions leading to complete communication failure. This feature of connected speech is studied under the heading juncture.

Thus, assimilation, elision, and juncture are the distinct features of connected speech about which a good deal of idea is very important for having a reasonably good command of spoken English. These concepts are very useful in making a scientific study of English on one hand, and adding to the intelligibility of a speaker as well as a listener, on the other hand.

Exercises

Q1. What is the difference between phonetics and phonology?

Q2. Draw a chart showing all the consonants of English along with their manner of articulation, place of articulation, and voicing.

Q3. Draw a diagram showing all the vowels of English with a view to classifying them.

Q4. Show the difference between these.

(a) Plosive sounds and Affricate sounds

(b) Velar sounds and Glottal sounds

(c) Bilabial fricative sound and Labio-dental fricative sound

(d) Close vowels and Open vowels

(e) Front vowels and Central vowels

(f) Phoneme and Allophone

(g) Complementary distribution and Contrastive distribution

(h) Phonetic transcription and Phonemic transcription

(i) Rising tone and Falling tone

(j) Stressed and Unstressed syllables

(k) Assimilation and Elision

Q5. Show your acquaintance with the following terms.

(a) Minimal pair (b) Phonetic environment

(c) Syllable (d) Aspiration

(e) Free variation (f) Stress

(g) Rhythm (h) Intonation

(i) Stress group (j) Pitch

(k) Juncture (l) Phonotactics

Q6. What do you mean by supra-segmental features?

Q7. What is phonemic transcription?

Q8. Phonemically transcribe the following words.

(a) Property (b) Straight

(c) Electricity (d) Geometrically

(e) Respiration (f) Ignorance

(g) Distributive (h) Verification

(i) Relativity (j) Generously

Q9. Mark the stress on the correct syllable of the words given in question number 8 and 10.

Q10. Identify and distinguish the syllables of the words given below.

(a) Syllabification (b) Mobility
(c) Normally (d) Grammatically
(e) Inclined (f) Borrowing
(g) Teacher (h) Respectfully
(i) Pollution (j) Laboratory

Morphology

7

7.1 What is Morphology?

Morphology is that branch of linguistics in which we study about words. Usually words are the groups of letters which are joined together to produce meaning, and so, these are considered as the meaningful units of a language. One word may have either one or more than one group of letters within it that can be identified on the basis of its meaning. For example, the word 'wise' has only one group of letters that gives one meaning, whereas the word 'unwise' has two groups of letters, 'un' and 'wise' and it gives a different meaning from the word wise in combination. These two groups of letters are distinguished on the basis of meaning that they produce in the internal constitution of the word 'unwise'. It shows that a word has one or more than one meaningful unit inside it that produces the meaning. In English, there are words like laws, lawful, lawfulness, unlawful, lawfully, etc. which have been derived from the source word 'law'. Hence, morphology deals with each meaningful unit of a word.

7.2 Some Important Concepts of Morphology

7.2.1 Morpheme

It is the smallest grammatical, meaningful unit of a language. It is that linguistic unit which exists either as a word or a constituent of a word. Look at these words and their constituents.

Possible	—	no constituent
Impossible	—	im - possible

Asocial — a - social
Boys — boy - s
Truthfulness — truth - ful - ness
Unfaithfulness — un - faith - ful - ness

Here all the constituents are morphemes as all of these affect the meaning of the word in some way or other. In some cases, the grammatical class of the word changes, and in others, the meaning changes to a certain extent after addition of morphemes. In some words, it changes the number or the gender as well. It will be discussed in detail in later part of this chapter. Conventionally, morphemes are placed under the braces like [ ].

7.2.2 Morph

It is the orthographic (written form) and subsequently phonetic realization of a morpheme, i.e. it is a physically identifiable morpheme. All the words that have one morpheme have essentially one morph. There are words like went, took, etc. which have two morphemes but one morph as two morphemes of these words are fused into one in such a way that they cannot be physically identified. Look at these words.

Went — go + past morpheme (- ed)

Took — take + past morpheme (- ed)

Liked — like + past morpheme (- ed)

We see that the past morphemes (- ed) of 'went' and 'took' are not visible or identifiable unlike the past morpheme (- ed) of 'liked'. Therefore, the word 'liked' has two morphemes and two morphs, but the words 'went' and 'took' have two morphemes and one morph each. There are words like 'sheep', 'deer', etc. which don't have plural forms. In such cases, the plural forms are technically called zero morph.

Sheep — sheep + zero morph

Deer — deer + zero morph

Such words also, have two morphemes but one morph, because plural morpheme is invisible in them. On this basis we can say that all morphs are morphemes but not all morphemes are morphs.

7.2.3 Allomorphs

These are the variants or alternative realizations of morphemes. That is to say, some morphemes are realized in different forms in different words, such as the plural morpheme [s] is realized as [s] in words like cats, caps, etc; it is realized as [z] in words like dogs, cubs, etc; it is realized as [iz] in words like nurses, judges, etc. All of these three forms [s], [z] and [iz] are allomorphs of the plural morpheme. It shows that an allomorph derives its identity on the basis of its placement in a distinct phonetic environment. The realization of these allomorphs is determined, thus, by a set of morphophonemic rules that we will see later in this chapter. Since allomorphs are also orthographically represented, they are all morphs but not all morphs are allomorphs as many morphs do not have alternative forms. It can better be understood with the help of the following diagram.

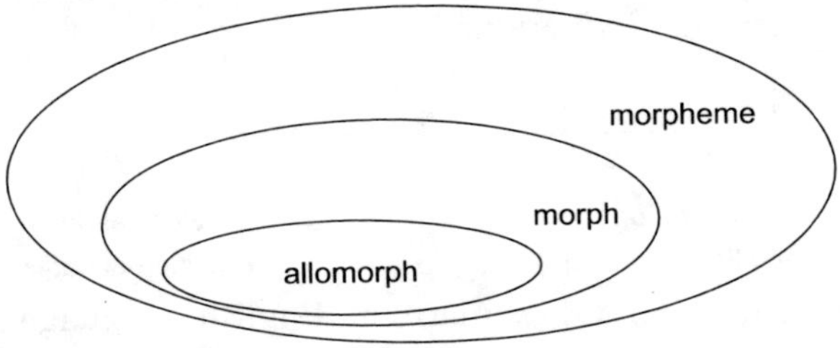

7.2.4 Lexeme

A lexeme is that fundamental form of a word in which it appears in a dictionary and works as the source of other forms of this word. For example, the word 'play' is a lexeme from which its inflected forms like plays, played, playing, are obtained. The inflectional range of the word 'play' in verbal form includes play, plays, played and playing, and so, the word play is lexeme that is realized in these many inflected forms in different contexts. Likewise, the words player, players, player's, players,' represent the inflectional paradigm of the lexeme 'player'. The word 'player' cannot be accommodated in the inflectional paradigm of the lexeme 'play' because of its reference to a different meaning along with difference in grammatical category and place in dictionary. Apart from this, the lexeme 'player' has its own inflectional paradigm. A lexeme, thus, may be treated as an abstract entity which is orthographically or phonologically manifested through the different word forms of its inflectional paradigm as shown above in the examples. On the basis of the explanation of lexeme, it can be said that all lexemes are words but not all words are lexemes.

7.2.5 Affixation

It is a process of addition of morphemes (affixes) to a word according to the grammatical (inflectional) or semantic (derivational) requirement in a particular context. For example, in a sentence 'Ali goes' the word 'go' is affixed (morpheme [es] is added) to get subject-verb agreement in the sentence. This affixation is grammatical requirement (inflectional). Likewise, we have words 'faithful' 'childhood' 'illogical', etc. in which affixation takes place according to the need of meaning (derivational). It can be seen like this.

Affixation

Prefixation (addition of prefix)

Suffixation (addition of suffix)

This affixation takes place in English language through prefixation or suffixation.

Prefixation is that process in which a morpheme is added in the beginning or initial position of a word. Such morphemes are called prefixes.

Suffixation is that in which a morpheme is added in the final position of a word. Such morphemes are called suffixes.

Look at these words.

Word	Root	Prefix	Suffix
Unlawful	Law	Un-	-ful
Illogical	Logic	Il-	-al
Boys	Boy	–	-s
Taken	Take	–	-en
Impolite	Polite	Im-	–

Thus, we see that root is that which can stand alone or exist at its own unlike prefixes and suffixes which cannot stand at their own as a word unless they are bound (affixed) to a root word. The examples given above clearly indicate that un-, -ful, il-, -s, -en, etc. are the affixes which cannot be used freely as words. On this basis, we can go for a generalization like all the root words are morphemes but not all the morphemes are root words.

7.3 Classification of Morphemes of English Language

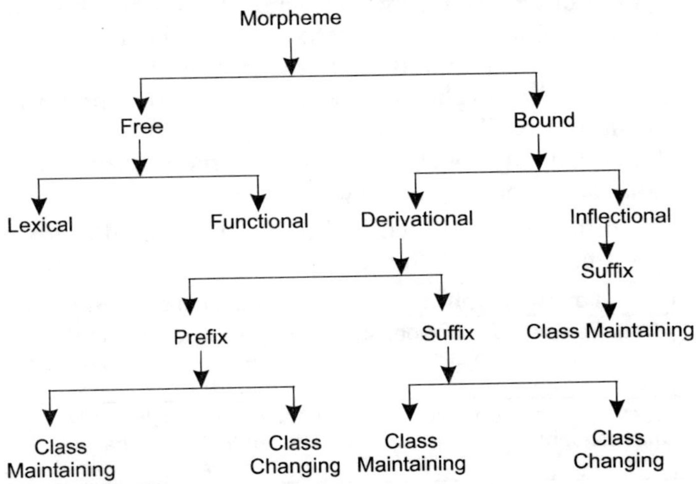

7.3.1 Free Morphemes and Bound Morphemes

Free morphemes are those root words which are used without affixes (suffix and prefix). These are the root words left after all affixes are removed from it. On the other hand, bound morphemes are those affixes which are always used in the company of free-morphemes. A free morpheme is a precondition for the use of a bound morpheme. All the prefixes and suffixes are bound morphemes, and the word to which they are attached, is free morpheme (the root word). For example, in the word 'unmerciful' 'un' and 'ful' are bound morphemes, while 'mercy' is free morpheme. These bound morphemes [un] and [ful] cannot be used without 'mercy' that may stand alone.

7.3.2 Lexical and Functional Morphemes

Lexical morphemes are those free morphemes which are open to affixation, i.e. affixes can be added to them as per the requirement. These are content words which give the main idea in a sentence. Such morphemes are nouns, verbs, adjectives, etc. that contain the central meaning in a sentence. The words like *boy, play, good, clever*, etc. are lexical morphemes as all of these words primarily add to the meaning of a sentence and they can be affixed as well.

On the other hand, functional morphemes are those which are not open to affixation, i.e. affixes cannot be added to them. They are usually required to fulfil grammatical functions in sentences. Such morphemes are auxiliary verbs, prepositions, conjunctions, etc. The words like *am, and, from, about,* etc. are functional morphemes as all of these basically serve grammatical purpose in sentences.

The differences between lexical and functional morphemes can be summarized as follows.

	Lexical morphemes	Functional morphemes
I.	They are open to affixation, and so, belong to open class of words.	They are close to affixation, and so, belong to closed class of words.
II.	They are phonologically independent.	They are phonologically dependent on lexical morphemes.
III.	They are usually stressed.	They are usually unstressed.
IV.	They are content words.	They are form words.
V.	They are usually polysyllabic.	They are usually monosyllabic.
VI.	They don't have grammatical features usually.	They have potential grammatical features.

7.3.3 Derivational and Inflectional Morphemes

Bound morphemes are of two kinds in English language, derivational and inflectional. Derivational bound morphemes are realized through prefixes as well as suffixes, whereas inflectional bound morphemes are realized through suffixes only. Inflectional morphemes are those which are used to fulfill the grammatical requirements. It is seen that nouns or verbs take different forms depending on person, number, tense, etc.

in sentences. For example, 'Salma goes to college', 'He talked to me', 'Two boys came' in all of these sentences, morphemes [es], [ed] and [s] work as present tense suffix (goes), past tense suffix (talked), and plural suffix (boys), respectively. There are three kinds of inflections used in English.

(a) Nominal inflections (affixed with nouns)—They are used as plural markers in words like *cats, dogs, mangoes*, etc., and as possessive markers (genitive) in words with apostrophe, such as *cat's, Ram's*, etc.

(b) Verbal inflections (affixed with verbs)—They are used as present tense marker in words like *goes, plays*, etc., as past tense marker in words like *worked, danced*, etc., as present participle marker in words like *going, walking*, etc. and as past participle marker in words like *taken, given*, etc.

(c) Adjectival inflections (affixed with adjectives)—They are used as comparative and superlative degree markers in words like greater, sweeter, greatest, sweetest, etc.

Altogether there are eight forms of inflections found in English which are represented by: -s, -'s (nominal), -s, -ed, -ing, -en (verbal), -er, -est (adjectival).

All of these inflectional suffixes basically serve the grammatical function in sentences. Inflectional suffixes are always used in the final position of a word. The grammatical class (parts of speech) of a word does not change after an inflectional suffix is added to it. Therefore, it is always class maintaining. Look at these words and their classes.

boy (noun) - boys (noun)	talk (verb) - talked (verb)
go (verb) - goes (verb)	great (adj) - greater (adj)

Derivational morphemes are those which are used to fulfil the semantic requirements in a particular context. These morphemes produce new words in terms of grammatical category and meaning from the original word. For example, the word 'bookish' that has [-ish] as derivational morpheme, is realized as a new word from 'book' and so, its class changes from noun (book) to adjective (bookish) along with change of meaning. Such morphemes are class changing. In some cases, the class of a word remains the same even after addition of a morpheme that is class maintaining. Further, more than one derivational suffix may be used in one word, such as, 'lawlessness' has two such morphemes [-less] and [-ness], one after the other. Such additions can go further in long words like 'democratizational', 'nationalistically', etc. When one word has both derivational and inflectional suffixes, derivational suffix is closer than the inflectional to the root word, e.g. writers, players, etc. in which [-er] is derivational morpheme followed by [-s] the inflectional morpheme.

The differences between the inflectional and derivational morphemes can be summarized as follows.

	Inflectional	Derivational
I.	It fulfills the grammatical necessity in a sentence.	It fulfills the semantic necessity in a sentence.
II.	It is always terminal (final) in position.	It may be initial, medial, or final in position.
III.	It doesn't change the class of the root, i.e. it is always class maintaining.	It may change the class of the root, i.e. it is class maintaining as well as class changing.
IV.	It doesn't alter the meaning of the word.	It alters the meaning of the word.
V.	It is limited in form.	It is diverse in form.

7.3.4 Class Changing and Class Maintaining Morphemes

Class changing and class maintaining are the two kinds of derivational morphemes. Class changing derivational morphemes are those that change the grammatical category (parts of speech) of the root after affixation. For example, the suffix '-able' changes the class of the word 'read' from verb to adjective 'readable'.

Look at these examples of class changing derivational morphemes.

Kill (verb)	Killer (noun)
Urban (adjective)	Urbanize (verb)
Law (noun)	Lawful (adjective)
Kind (adjective)	Kindness (noun)

Class maintaining derivational morphemes are those that do not cause the change of grammatical class of the root after affixation. The suffixes -hood, -dom, -ess, -ship, etc. are the examples that can be seen in the words given below.

Child (noun)	Childhood (noun)
King (noun)	Kingdom (noun)
Lion (noun)	Lioness (noun)
Friend (noun)	Friendship (noun)

All the examples given above show that it is suffixation that has brought about the changes in the root words.

Likewise, prefixation also results into class changing and class maintaining morphemes that can be seen through these examples.

Political (adj.)	Apolitical (adj.)	Class maintaining prefixes
Metre (noun)	Pentametre (noun)	
Behave (verb)	Misbehave (verb)	
Sleep (verb)	Asleep (adj.)	Class changing prefixes
Grade (noun)	Degrade (verb)	
Little (adj.)	Belittle (verb)	

7.3.5 Some Important Prefixes and Suffixes in English

Prefixes and suffixes play a very crucial role in derivation of the meaning of words wherever they are used. The process of derivation has been one of the most important sources of word formation in the English language. It has considerably enriched this language in terms of vocabulary. A good idea of prefixes and suffixes is very essential to have a good command of English words. Therefore, let us talk about some important prefixes and suffixes used in English.

7.3.5.1 Prefixes frequently used

I. Number prefixes

Prefix	Meaning	Words
Mono-	One	Monometer, Unicellular
Uni-		
Bi-	Two	Bipolar, Diglossia
di-		

Tri-	Three	Trilateral, Trilingual
Tetra-	Four	Tetrameter, Tetra-syllabic
Penta-	Five	Penta-cyclic, Pentametric
Hexa-	Six	Hexamorphic, Hexameter
Hepta-	Seven	Heptameter, Heptasyllabic
Octa-	Eight	Octasyllabic, Octametre
Nano-	Nine	Nanomorphic, Nanosyllabic
Deca-	Ten	Decameter, Decasyllabic
Multi-		
Poly-	Many	Multilingual, Polyclinic

II. Prefixes related to scientific study

Astro-	**Related to stars**	**Astrology, Astrophysics**
Bio-	Related to life	Biology, Biochemistry
Cosmo-	Related to universe	Cosmology
Cardio-	Related to heart	Cardiology, Cardiography
Geo-	Related to earth	Geology, Geography
Hydro-	Related to water	Hydrology
Photo-	Related to light	Photography
Thermo-	Related to heat	Thermodynamics
Socio-	Related to society	Sociology
Osteo-	Related to bone	Osteology
Physio-	Related to body	Physiology
Psycho-	Related to mind	Psychology
Neuro-	Related to nerves	Neurology
Zoo-	Related to animals	Zoology

III. Prefixes related to time

Ante-	Before	Antenatal, Antediluvian
Ex-	Former	Ex-chairman, Ex-minister
Fore-	Before	Forecast, Foretell
Pre-	Before	Prefix, Pre-examination
Post-	After	Post-colonial, Post-romantic
Neo-	New	Neo-classical, Neo-cultural
Re-	Again	Rebuild, Remake

IV. Prefixes related to size

Ab-	Unexpected	Abnormal
Mini-	Small	Minibus, Mini-matters

Hyper-	More	Hypersensitive, Hyperactive
Hypo-	Less	Hypoglycemia, Hypothyroidism
Micro-	Small	Microbiology, Micro-study
Macro-	Big	Macroeconomics, Macro-mechanics
Sub-	Below	Sub-inspector, Sub-class
Ultra-	Beyond	Ultramodern, Ultrasound
Under-	Within	Underestimate, Underfed
Intra-	Within	Intra-lingual, Intra-national
Inter-	Out	Inter-lingual, International

V. Prefixes related to negation

A-	Not	Apolitical, Asocial
Dis-	Not	Dislike, Disagree
De-	Not	Defame, Decode
In-	Not	Incomplete, Indigestion
Im-	Not	Impolite, Impossible
Il-	Not	Illogical, Illegal
Ir-	Not	Irrelevant, Irrational
Mis-	Not	Mislead, Misguide
Non-	Not	Non-political, Non-technical
Un-	Not	Ungrammatical, Unmanageable
Mal-	Not	Malnutrition, Malfunction

VI. Some miscellaneous prefixes

Anti-	Against	Anti-national, Anti-social
Pro-	In support of	Pro-government, Pro-student
Super-	Extra ordinary	Superman, Supernatural
Over-	Extra	Overflow, Overgrowth
Out-	Away	Outhouse, Outpost
Tele-	Far	Telescope, Telephone
Co-	Together	Co-education, Co-existence
Counter-	Against	Counterproductive, Counteract
Pan-	All over	Pan-Indian, Pan-Libyan

7.3.5.2 Suffixes frequently used

I. Suffixes used to form nouns

Suffix	Words
-ance	Attendance, Assistance
-ant	Assistant, Pollutant

Suffix	Words
-ation	Information, Confirmation
-an	Indian, Libyan
-acy	Delicacy, Bureaucracy
-ary	Secondary, Dictionary
-age	Mileage, Pilgrimage
-ar	Liar, Beggar
-er	Player, Teacher
-or	Director, Inspector
-ee	Employee, Refugee
-dom	Kingdom, Dukedom
-ess	Lioness, Tigress
-hood	Childhood, Falsehood
-ism	Populism, Nationalism
-eer	Engineer, Profiteer
-ness	Wickedness, Kindness
-let	Starlet, Booklet
-ment	Government, Development
-ist	Nationalist, Artist
-ity	Popularity, Regularity
-ion	Correction, Relation
-ence	Dependence, Excellence
-ship	Kingship, Friendship
-sion	Admission, Conclusion
-ty	Cruelty, Penalty
-ure	Failure, Pleasure

II. Suffixes used to form adjectives

-able	Suitable, Honourable
-al	Personal, National
-an	Asian, European
-ar	Tabular, Rectangular
-ate	Fortunate, Duplicate
-ary	Necessary, Customary
-ible	Horrible, Terrible
-ish	Boyish, Childish
-ive	Attentive, Productive
-ic	Terroristic, Nationalistic

-ous	Famous, Nervous
-ific	Horrific, Terrific
-less	Flawless, Careless
-eous	Beauteous, Gaseous
-like	Childlike, Manlike
-some	Troublesome, Quarrelsome
-ly	Friendly, Cowardly
-worthy	Praiseworthy, Trustworthy
-wise	Classwise, Agewise
-ful	Beautiful, Useful
-ed	Talented, Educated
-y	Dirty, Oily

III. Suffixes used to form verbs

-en	Strengthen, Darken
-ize	Capitalize, Nationalize
-ify	Classify, Terrify
-nate	Hyphenate, Chlorinate
-ed	Talked, Bombed

IV. Suffixes used to form adverbs

-wards	Northwards, Backwards
-wise	Likewise, Framewise
-ly	Wisely, Carefully

7.4 Identification of Morphemes

Any word consists of either one morpheme or more than one morpheme. A word that has one morpheme (free morpheme) is called monomorphic word. Likewise, words with many morphemes are called polymorphic words. As we have come to know that each morpheme has its effect on the meaning of the word, it is important to identify the morphemes as constituents of words in order to know their meaning properly. It helps us in enriching our vocabulary and developing an insight into the meanings of words as well. The identification of morphemes enables us to predict the meaning of a word to a great extent. In this regard, it is important to mention that a word is realized in different forms when its morphemes are divided. These different forms have been categorized as root, stem, and base. Therefore, let us have a look at these terms.

7.4.1 The Concepts of Root, Stem and Base

A **root** is that free morpheme to which any other morpheme (bound) is affixed. It is that morpheme which remains as a word after all affixes are removed. For example, in the word 'anti-national' 'anti-' and '-al' are affixes (prefix and suffix), while 'nation' is the root as 'nation' will be left after removal of these two affixes and it can stand as a word alone.

A stem is that part of a word which remains after an inflectional suffix is removed from it. That is to say, any form to which an inflectional suffix can be added may be called stem. The words 'teach' and 'teacher' may be realized as stems as they can be affixed with inflectional suffixes '-es' and '-s' respectively. The word 'teach' may be a root as well as a stem, but the word 'teacher' will be a stem only, not a root. Likewise, in the word 'non-technicians' 'non-technician' is a stem after removal of the plural suffix '-s'. Thus, the concept of stem is associated with inflectional feature.

A base is that form of a word which is open to affixation of any kind, inflectional or derivational. For example, in the word 'traditionalists' 'traditionalist' is a stem as well as a base because inflectional suffix '-s' has been added to it, but 'traditional' is a base, not a stem because it can be affixed with derivational suffix '-ist' only. Likewise, the word 'tradition' is a base because it can be affixed; it is a stem because it can be inflected; it is a root because it does not have a bound morpheme. Thus, it can be said that the same word may belong to all three classes; root, stem and base depending on the characteristics mentioned above. The difference among these terms is observable and relevant in making morphological analysis of words.

7.4.2 Tree-diagrams of Morphemes

The morphemic constituents of a word may be presented through a diagram step by step. It will show how affixation takes place and what changes occur at different levels in terms of meaning and grammatical category.

(I) unpopular

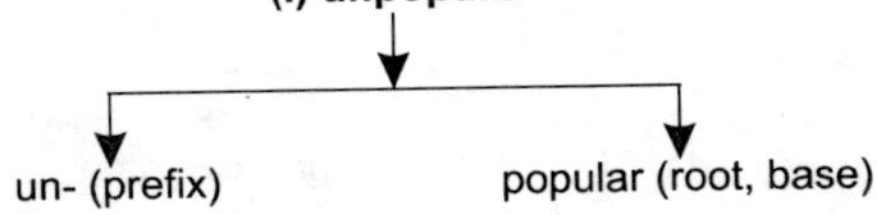

(II) carelessness

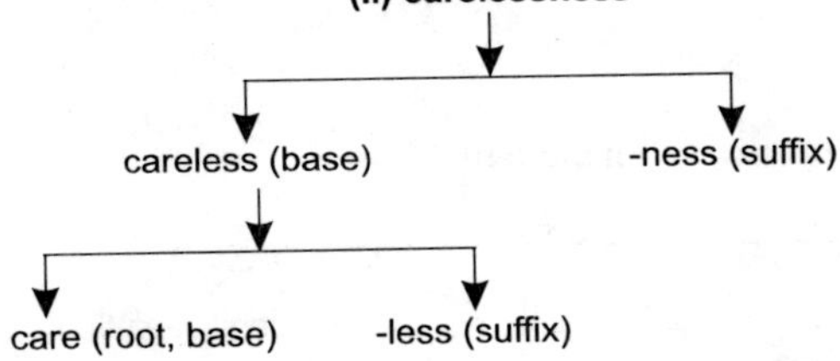

(III) unbelievable

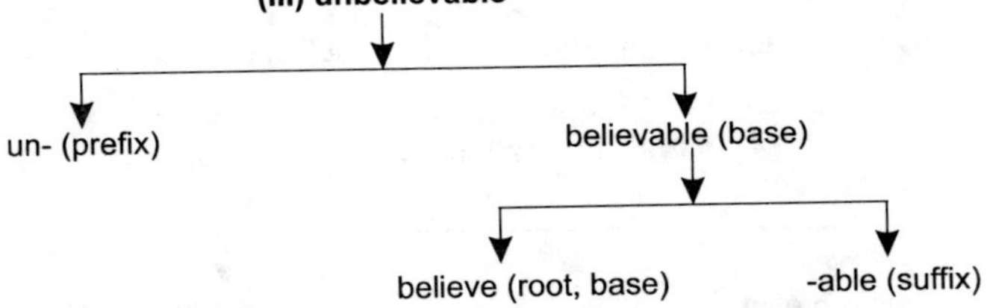

(IV) foolishness

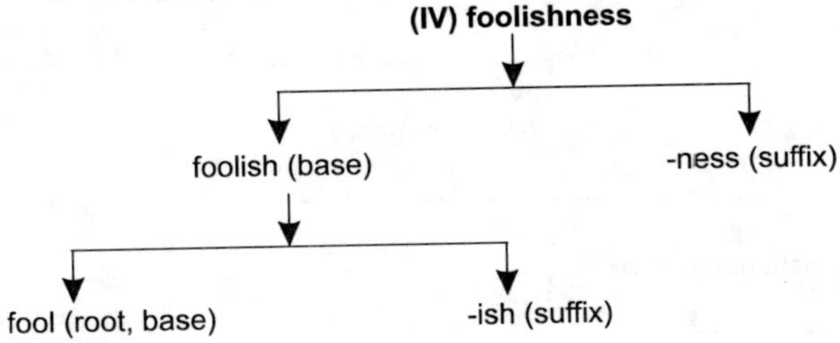

(V) players

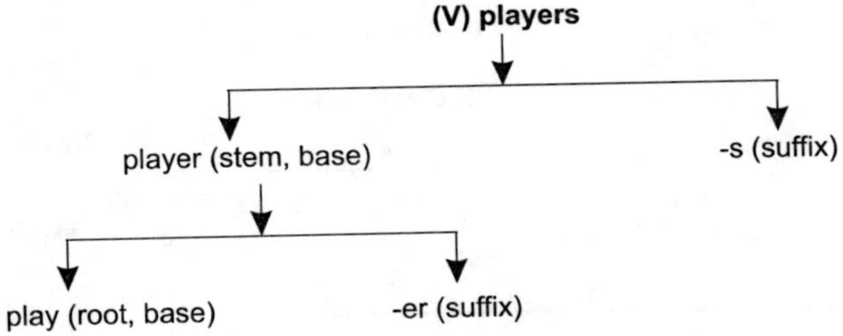

(VI) apolitical

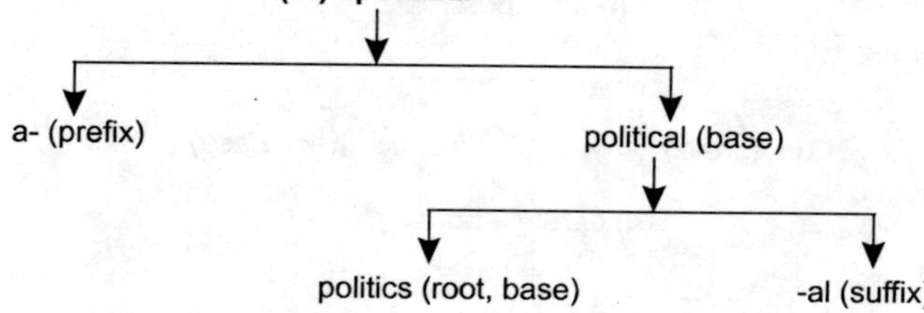

(VII) students'

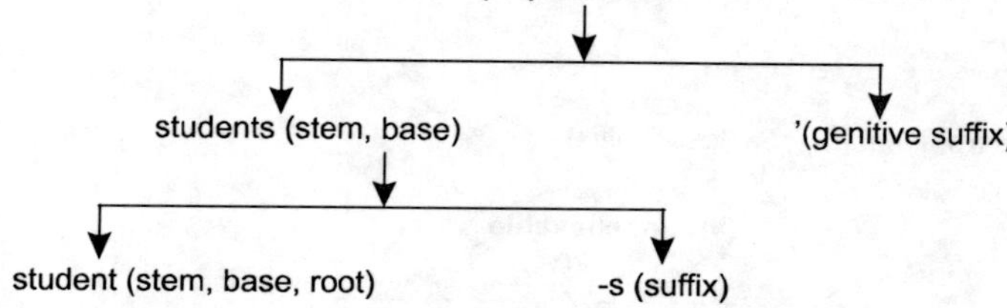

(VIII) anti-nationalists

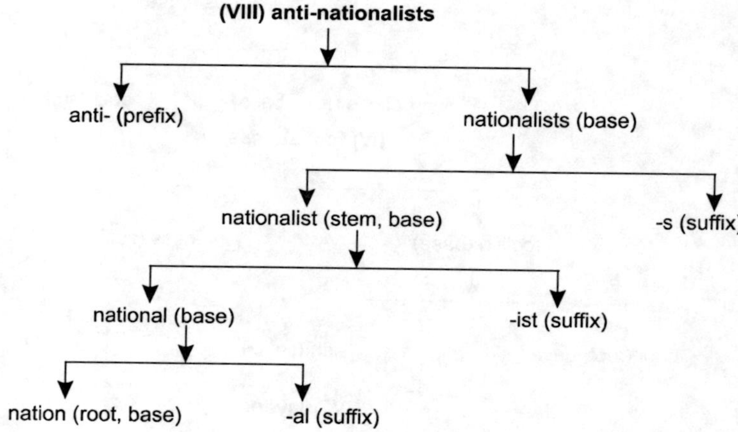

(IX) stabilization

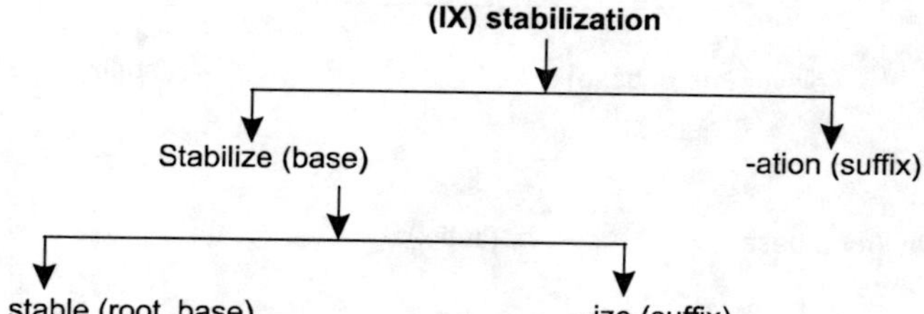

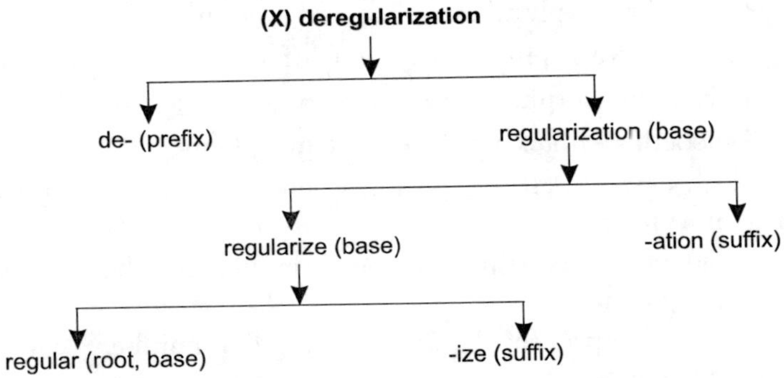

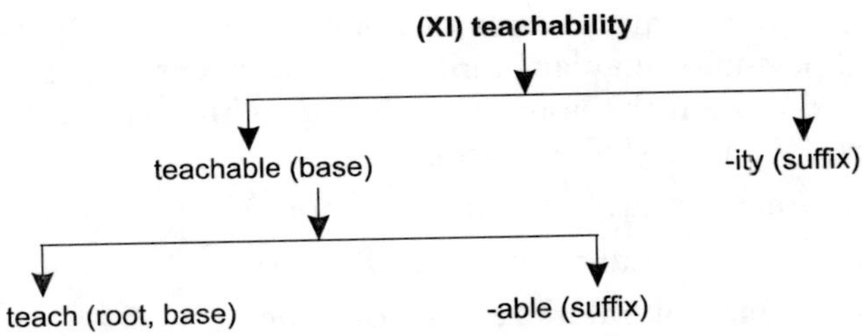

All of these tree-diagrams clearly indicate the constituent morphemes of words given above. At each level of analysis (division) we find the change in the grammatical category and subsequently in the meaning of the word. It is really very useful in understanding the internal constitution of a word.

7.5 Morphophonemics

Morphophonemics deals with the phonological aspect of morphemes. It is, therefore, that branch of linguistics which is in between phonology and morphology. We study the phonetic realizations of different forms of morphemes in it. How different morphemes, particularly inflectional suffixes, are pronounced in different words, constitutes the subject matter of morphophonemics. It lays down several rules that may be seen as follows.

(I) The plural morphemes of nouns, genitive morphemes, and third person—singular number—present tense morphemes (verbs) are realized as /s/ if the noun or verb ends with a voiceless sound except /s/, /ʃ/ and /tʃ/. For example:

Cats - /kæts/ (plural morpheme of a noun)

Cups - /kΛps/ (plural morpheme of a noun)

Locks - /lɒks/ (plural morpheme of a noun)

Macbeth's - /mækbeɵs/ (genitive morpheme)

Writes - /raIts/ (third person – singular number – present tense morpheme)

Speaks - /spi:ks/ (third person – singular number – present tense morpheme)

Hops - /hɒps/ (third person – singular number – present tense morpheme)

(II) The plural morphemes of nouns, genitive morphemes, and third person – singular number – present tense morphemes are realized as /z/ if the noun or verb ends with a voiced sound except /z/, /ʒ/ and /dʒ/. For example:

Dogs - /dɒgz/ (plural morpheme of noun)

Pens - /penz/ (plural morpheme of noun)

Balls - /bɔ:lz/ (plural morpheme of noun)

Abdul's - /əbdulz/ (genitive suffix)

Moves - /mu:vz/ (third person – singular number – present tense)

Runs - /rΛnz/ (third person – singular number – present tense)

Climbs - /klaImz/ (third person – singular number – present tense).

(III) The plural morphemes of nouns, genitive morphemes, and third person – singular number – present tense morphemes are realized as /Iz/ if the noun or verb ends with /s/, /z/, /ʃ/, /ʒ/, /tʃ/or /dʒ/. For examples:

Judges - /dʒΛdʒIz/

Rouges - /ru:ʒIz/

Buses - /bΛsIz/

Churches - /tʃə:tʃIz/ plural morpheme of a noun)

Prince's - /prInsIz/ (genitive morpheme)

Tosses - /tƆ:sIz/ (third person – singular number – present tense)

Fetches - /fetʃIz/ (third person – singular number – present tense)

Flashes - /flæʃIz/ (third person – singular number – present tense)

Buzzes - /bΛzIz/.

(IV) The past tense morpheme [-ed] is realized as /t/ when a verb ends with a voiceless sound except /t/. For example:

Talked - /tƆ:kt/

Stopped - /stɒpt/

Tossed - /tɒst/

Dashed - /dæʃt/

Matched - /mætʃt/

Laughed - /la:ft/.

(V) The past tense morpheme [-ed] is realized as /d/ when a verb ends with a voiced sound except /d/. For example:

Bombed - /bɒmd/

Dragged - /drægd/

Pained - /peInd/

Killed - /kIld/

Moved - /mu:vd/

Tamed - /teImd/.

(VI) The past tense morpheme [-ed] is realized as /Id/ when a verb ends with either /t/ or /d/. For example:

Wanted - /wa:ntId/

Shouted - /ʃautId/

Started - /sta:tId/

Ended - /endId/

Landed - /lændId/

Mended - /mendId/.

Thus, we find that the same orthographic form of morphemes is phonetically realized in different forms. It is very important to know these rules in order to pronounce such morphemes correctly in different words.

7.6 Formation of Words in English Language

Right from the days of the origin of a language, new words keep on coming to its kitty in several ways. With advancement of society in which a particular language is used, the need of new expressions is felt. To fulfil this requirement, new words are coined or borrowed from other languages. The English language that has undoubtedly acquired the status of international language of the modern world has constantly enriched itself by addition of new words. These new words are formed by various processes that may be seen one by one.

(I) Compounding: It is that process of word formation in which two words are joined together to produce a new word. Compounding produces almost all classes of words right from the noun to interjection. There are many words formed by this process in English.

Examples

Text + book = textbook (noun)

Him + self = himself (pronoun)

Man + made = man-made (adjective)

Over + haul= overhaul (verb)

Care + fully = carefully (adverb)

In + to = into (preposition)

How + ever = however (conjunction)

Heigh + ho = heigh-ho (interjection)

(II) Derivation: When new words are formed by affixation, i.e. through addition of suffixes and prefixes, the process is called derivation. This is a very common process of word formation.

Examples

Un + popular = unpopular

Im + polite = impolite

Law + less = lawless

Boy + hood = boyhood

(III) Conversion: In this process, the class of a word changes without change in spelling. That is to say, when the same word is used in two ways conforming to two grammatical categories, the process is called conversion.

Examples

Love (noun)	Copy (noun)
Love (verb)	Copy (verb)
Train (noun)	Pain (noun)
Train (verb)	Pain (verb)

(IV) Duplication: It is that process in which a new word is formed by repetition of a word with changes in either its initial or medial sound.

Examples

Hotch-potch (change in its initial sound)

Dilly-dally (change in its medial sound)

Helter-skelter (change in its initial sound)

Nitty-gritty (change in its initial sound)

(V) Back-formation: When a new word is formed by the deletion of suffixes of some words, the process is called back-formation. The class of the new word is different from the class of the source word.

Examples

Supervisor – supervise (new word)
(noun) (verb)

Television – televise (new word)
(noun) (verb)

Enthusiasm – enthuse (new word)
(noun) (verb)

(VI) Clipping: It is that process in which a new word is formed by removal of some parts of a long word. That is to say, when a long word is cut to size without any change in its meaning and class, the process is called clipping.

Examples

Telephone – phone (initial part is clipped)

Laboratory – lab (terminal part is clipped)

Influenza – flu (both initial and terminal parts are clipped)

(noun) (noun)

Here we see that the grammatical class (that is noun here) of the source word and the new word remains the same. This makes clipping different from the back-formation.

(VII) Acronymy: The process in which the first letters of a group of words are put together to produce a new word is called acronymy.

Examples

UNO – United Nations Organization

BBC – British Broadcasting Corporation

NATO – North Atlantic Treaty Organization

(VIII) Blending: When initial part of one word and final part of another word are combined, a new word is formed. The process involved is called blending.

Examples

Breakfast + lunch = brunch
Smoke + fog = smog
Motor + hotel = motel
} New words

(IX) Multiple formation: It is that process in which two processes of word formation are used one after the other to make a new word. The first process is clipping and the second one is derivation.

Examples

(a) handkerchief $\xrightarrow{\text{(clipping)}}$ hank

Hank + -y $\xrightarrow{\text{(derivation)}}$ hanky

(b) nightgown $\xrightarrow{\text{(clipping)}}$ night

Night + -y $\xrightarrow{\text{(derivation)}}$ nighty

(X) Onomatopoeia: Some words are formed to convey certain sounds produced in nature. The articulation of such words suggests their meaning in terms of sound. Here, the source of word formation is the sound itself that occurs in nature. This process of word formation is called onomatopoeia. The words like gurgle, howling, burbling, etc. are its examples as these words automatically suggest their relationship with certain sounds.

Thus, all these processes are used to form new words in the English language. Although we talked about these many processes of word formation that account for many words of English, there are still a large number of words which cannot be explained in terms of these processes. It shows that there is further ample scope for research in this field.

Exercises

Q1. What do you mean by morphology?

Q2. What is affixation and what are its types?

Q3. Make five words with each of the prefixes given below.

Pre-	Neo-	Tri-	Psycho-
a-	Anti-	Non-	De-
Ir-	Il-	In-	Im-
Re-	Dis-	Uni-	Multi-

Q4. Make five words with each of the suffixes given below.

-ish	-able	-ity	-ify
-ous	-y	-ence	-dom
-eer	-ie	-ary	-or
-ness	-ee	-wards	-ize

Q5. Show the difference between these terms.

(a) morpheme and morph

(b) inflectional and derivational morphemes

(c) morpheme and allomorph

(d) prefix and suffix

(e) lexeme and word

(f) free morpheme and bound morphemes
(g) lexical and functional morpheme
(h) class changing and class maintaining morphemes
(i) root and stem
(j) back-formation and clipping

Q6. What is morphophonemics? Write down its important rules.

Q7. What is word formation? Write about the different processes of word formation in English language.

Q8. Draw tree-diagrams to show different morphemes of the following words along with the labels like root, base and stem.

(a) Monopolization	(b) De-establishment
(c) Republicanism	(d) Unconventional
(e) Neo-classicism	(f) Reinvestment
(g) Penta-syllabic	(h) Marketeer's
(i) Horrifying	(j) Immorality

(See the answers after the last chapter)

Q9. Look at the following words carefully and identify the process involved in their formation.

(a) Play	(b) Unresolved
(c) Classroom	(d) Motel
(e) Oxbridge	(f) IMF
(g) Telecast	(h) Comfy
(i) Helter-skelter	(j) Fridge
(k) Behave	(l) Goldmines
(m) Inform	(n) Nitty-gritty
(o) Over-burdened	

(See the answers after the last chapter)

Q10. Tick the right column which indicates the phonological realization of the inflectional morphemes in the following words. The first one has been done.

Words	s	z	Iz	t	d	Id
Boys		✓				
Wanted						
Shocked						
Abdul's						
Locked						
Bushes						
Colleges						
Handed						
Writers						
Words						
Noted						
Prince's						
Ladies						
Looked						
Painted						
Nurses						

(Check the answers with the help of a dictionary.)

Syntax

8

8.1 What is Syntax?

As morphology deals with words, syntax deals with sentences. A sentence is the largest grammatical unit that gives a complete sense, and so, syntax talks about all of its constituents like words, phrases and clauses in detail. Syntax deals with the analysis of all the components of a sentence that lead to the formation of a meaningful unit. How words are arranged in a particular order to produce a meaningful grammatical structure as a sentence is the subject matter of syntax. What makes a sentence like 'Ali plays football' an acceptable grammatical structure, while the other combinations of the same words like 'plays Ali football', 'plays football Ali' or 'football plays Ali' unacceptable grammatical structures is the field of investigation for syntax.

8.2 The Constituents of a Sentence

The constituents of a sentence mean all parts that contribute in producing the meaning. Since phrases and clauses are the grammatical units into which a sentence is divided, it is convenient to analyze it in terms of two parts (i) Phrasal constituents and (ii) Clausal constituents.

8.2.1 Phrasal Constituents

Words are the smallest units of a sentence which are placed in groups according to certain rules to produce a meaningful structure. Within a sentence, there are groups of words. These groups are found on the basis of semantic features of individual words that constitute it. That is to say, the sentence has layers of structures embedded inside it and all of these produce together the meaning of the structure.

When we look at the sentence 'The good boys should be rewarded' our attention naturally goes to two units 'the good boys' and 'should be rewarded' in terms of meaning. We don't think of the units like 'the good' and 'boys should be rewarded' or any other possible combination, as it sounds unnatural or incompatible. This semantic realization of the units of a sentence has given birth to the idea of phrase. A phrase that is a group of words gives partial meaning of a sentence and helps a reader in identifying the meaningful units that constitute sentences. Based on it, we have phrasal constituents of a sentence like Noun phrase, Verb phrase, Adjective phrase, Adverb phrase and Prepositional phrase. In a noun phrase, noun is the head word, and likewise we have all other phrases given above with the head words belonging to that category. For example, look at this sentence.

'The most intelligent students of my class speak very confidently'. All of these phrases can be seen like this.

Noun phrase (NP) – 'The most intelligent students of my class'

Verb phrase (VP) – 'speak very confidently'

Adjective phrase (Adj. Ph) – 'most intelligent'

Adverb phrase (Adv. Ph) – 'very confidently'

Prepositional phrase (PP) – 'of my class'

Here we see that adjective phrase, adverb phrase and prepositional phrase are all parts of noun phrase and verb phrase. An adjective phrase is a combination of a degree word and an adjective. An adverb phrase is a combination of a degree word and an adverb. A prepositional phrase is a combination of a preposition and a noun phrase.

It can further be seen through this sentence.

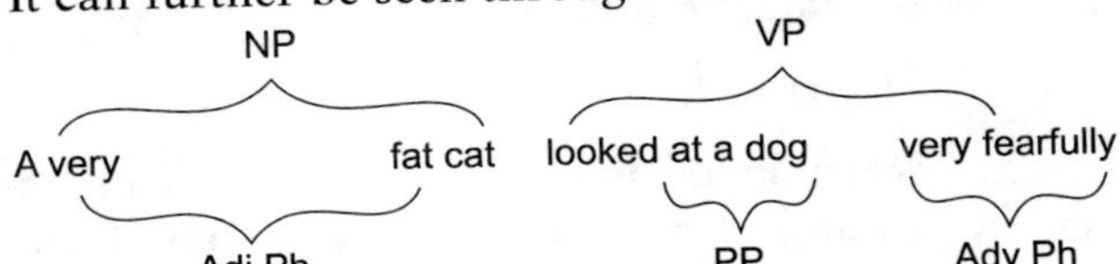

The analysis of this sentence shows that any formal sentence can logically be divided into two bigger units Noun phrase and Verb phrase, and other phrases exist as the constituents of these two units. These two bigger units are the essential constituents of a formal sentence, whereas other phrases are optional ones.

Now let us talk about all the possible constituents of an NP. The constituents of an NP can be represented through this diagram.

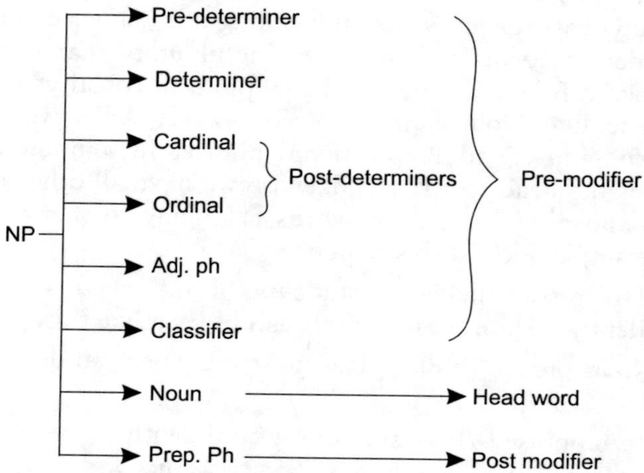

A noun that is the head word of an NP is its obligatory constituent and all other constituents are optional constituents which may or may not be found. All the words that precede the head word are called pre-modifiers, and those which follow it are called post-modifiers. Look at this structure.

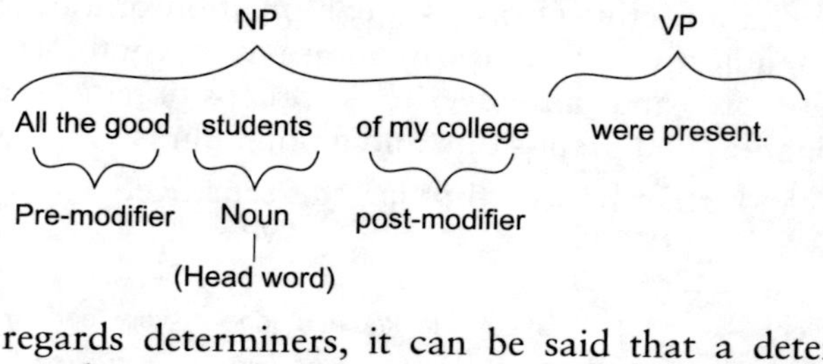

As regards determiners, it can be said that a determiner determines the coming of a noun in an NP. Apart from it, a determiner gives the information about noun that it modifies, in terms of its possession (whom does it belong to?), quantity (how much/many is it?), particularization (who/what is it?), etc. Thus a determiner establishes, to a great extent, the identity of a noun in the due course of modifying it. The words of grammatical categories such as, articles (a, an, the), possessives (my, your, our, Ali's), demonstratives (this, those, that), quantifiers (some, many, a lot of, much, ordinal and cardinal numbers, etc.), interrogative adjectives (which, what, whose, etc.), are considered as determiners. When more than one determiner occurs in an NP, we classify them as pre-determiner or post-determiner depending on the place they get in relation to the central determiners which are usually articles, possessives and demonstratives. These determiners like adjectives modify nouns, but there are differences between them that can be seen in the following ways.

Determiner	Adjective
I. It has no variable forms.	It has variable forms like positive, comparative and superlative.
II. It always comes before a noun that means as attributive.	It comes before as well as after a noun that means both as attributive and predicative.
III. Two determiners of the same kind cannot be used in an NP.	Two adjectives of the same kind can be used in an NP.
IV. A determiner always comes before an adjective if both occur in an NP.	An adjective always comes after a determiner if both occur in an NP.

Moreover, cardinals and ordinals are the numbers considered as post-determiners because they occur after the central determiners or regular determiners. When a determiner gives the idea of quantity, it is called quantifier. Usually, pre-determiners and cardinals appear as quantifiers in an NP. Further, a classifier as a constituent of NP is a word that occurs in the form of a noun and modifies the head word (noun). It always comes just before the head noun in an NP.

Now let us look at the following sentences and analyze the constituents of their noun phrases.

In these analyses, pre-determiner and determiner have been used in abbreviated forms as 'Pre-det' and 'Det' respectively.

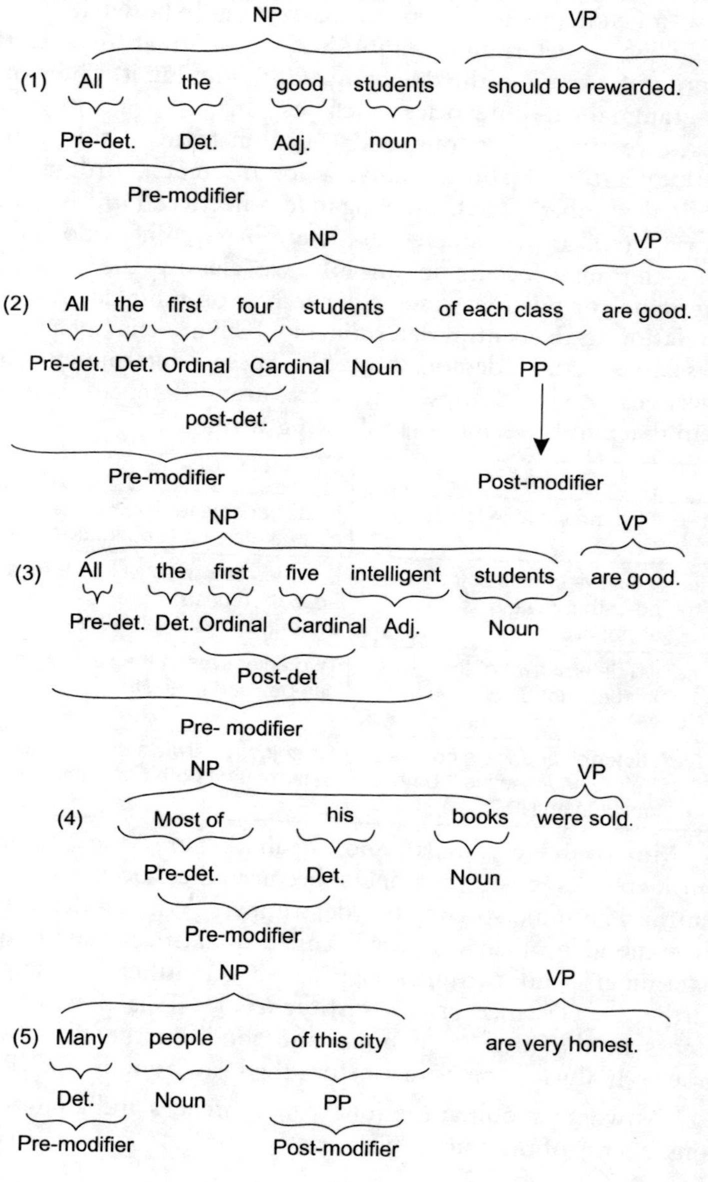

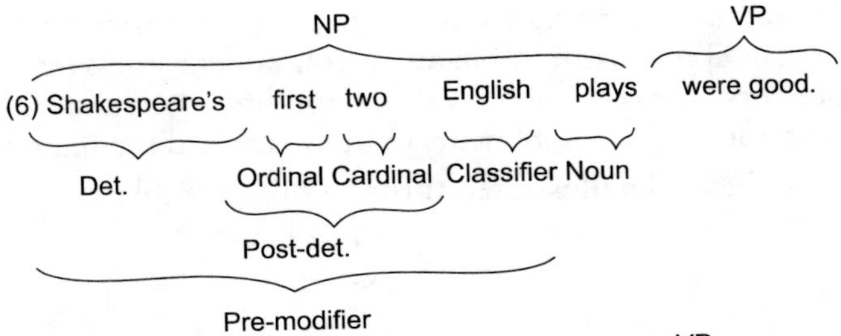

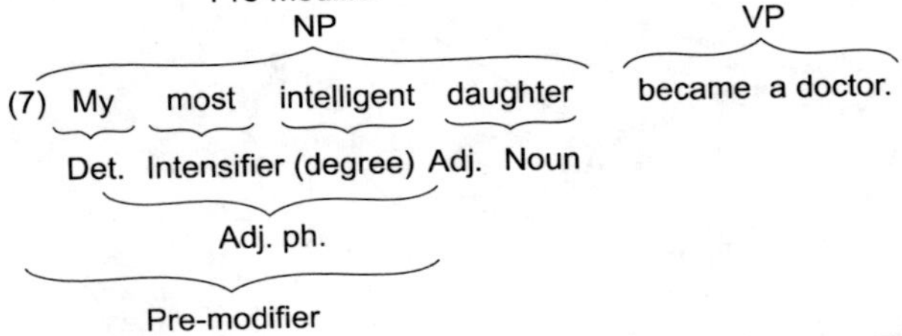

All of these sentences given above contain some of the constituents of an NP, but a noun appears as the essential constituent without which an NP is not possible. A pre-determiner is the first word in the list of pre-modifiers before which no other modifier of the head word can occur. A prepositional phrase occurs as the post-modifier in an NP. The words expressing degree of the adjectives or adverbs are considered as intensifiers.

After an NP, it is VP that constitutes the important string of a sentence. VP tells us about the tense of a sentence. A VP has basically two parts—auxiliary and main (lexical). It is usually the auxiliary verb that introduces the main verb. The components of a VP may be seen like this.

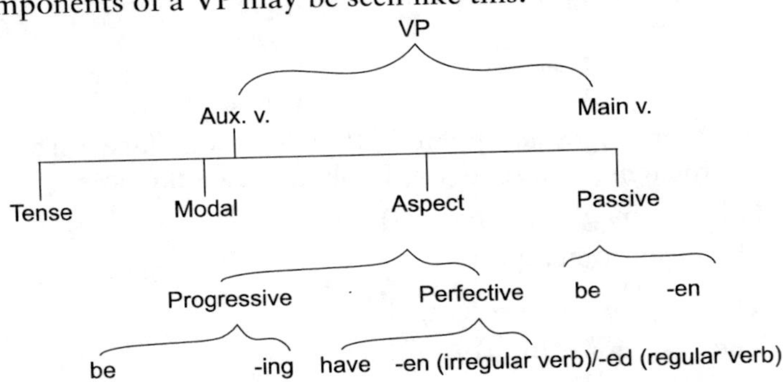

An auxiliary verb may have any of these components apart from tense. Tense is the obligatory component and rest of the components are optional. VP in totality is realized as a combination of the components of auxiliary and the main verb.

It can better be illustrated through this example.

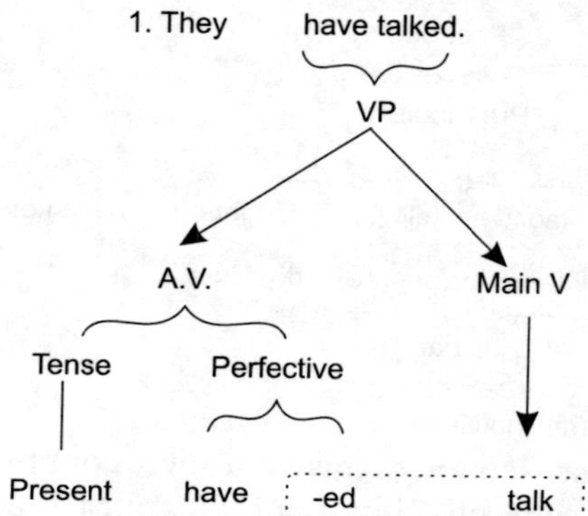

Here the form of the tense is realized through auxiliary 'have', that is present, and 'ed' component of perfective aspect goes to 'talk' to produce 'talked'. It is relevant to mention in this context that we have two tenses—present and past in English language based on the form of auxiliary verbs.

It can be seen like this.

Present		**Past**
Is	Be	Was
Are		Were
Am		Was
May		Might
Can		Could
Shall		Should
Will		Would

Another important point is that it is auxiliary verb that decides the tense of a sentence. Look at these sentences.

Nillu is going. (present)
Nillu was going. (past)

They have gone. (present)
They had gone. (past)

It is clear from these sentences that it is auxiliary verb that decides the tense of a sentence because main verbs are the same in both the given sets of sentences.

Now it is important to make a difference between tense and time. Tense is decided on the basis of the form of verbs as shown above, whereas time is considered for the derivation of the meaning from the sentence. Tense is exclusively a grammatical concept, whereas time is non-grammatical. Tense of a sentence may be present, while its time may refer to future. For example, in the sentence:

'Alok is going to Delhi tomorrow'.

(tense is present, time is future)

In the light of these observations, let us look at the components of the verb phrases of these sentences.

(1) They come.

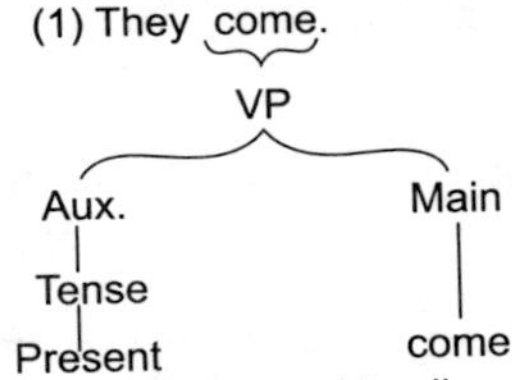

(2) He is good to all.

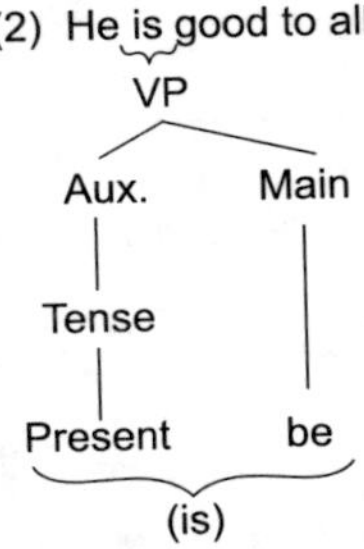

(3) Saroj is going.

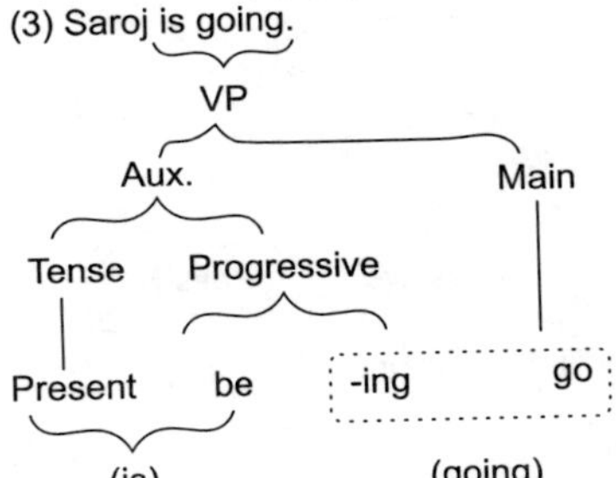

(4) I may go.

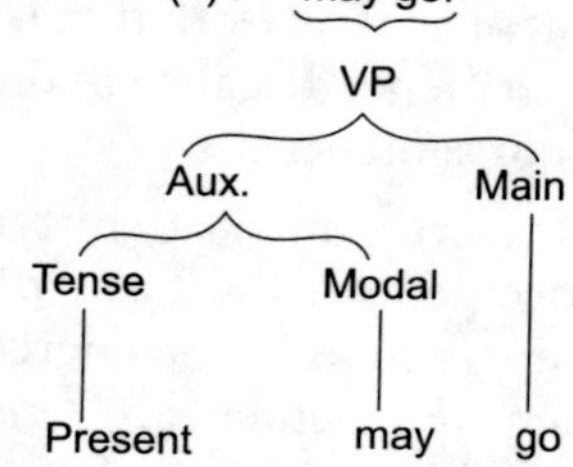

(5) Ashok may have gone.

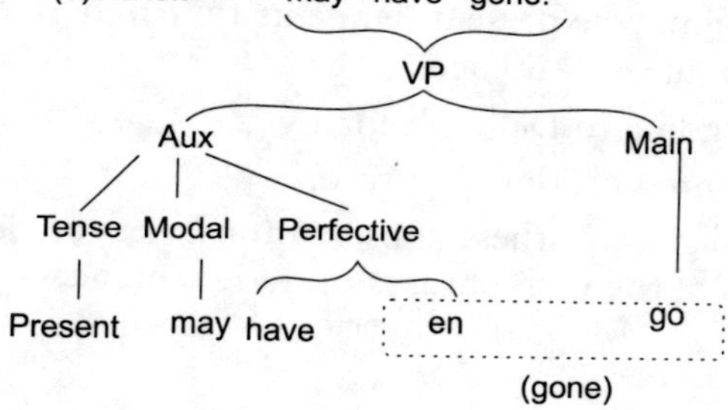

(6) She might have been going.

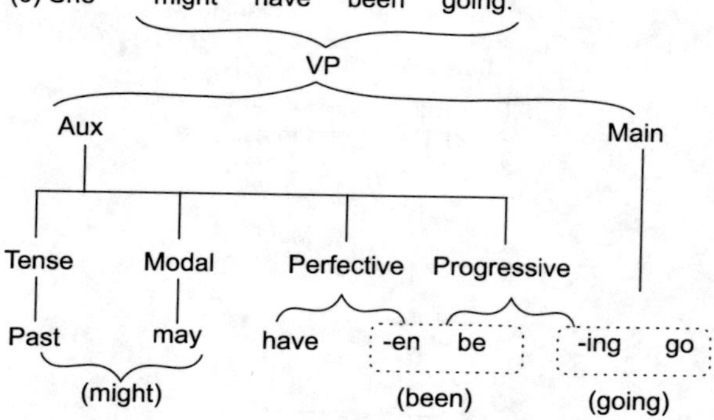

(7) They are being taken to hospital.

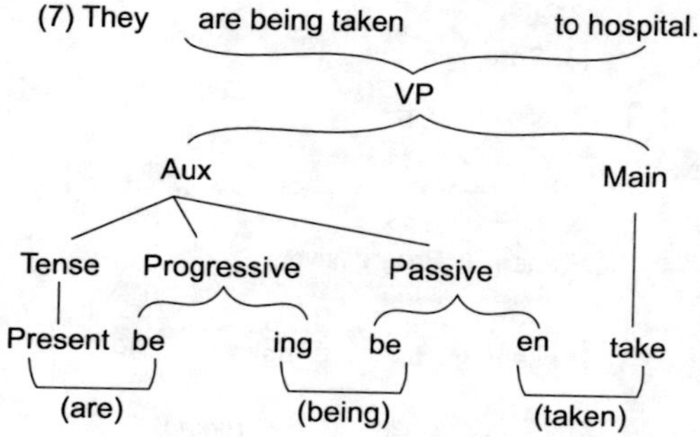

(8) They may have been being repaired.

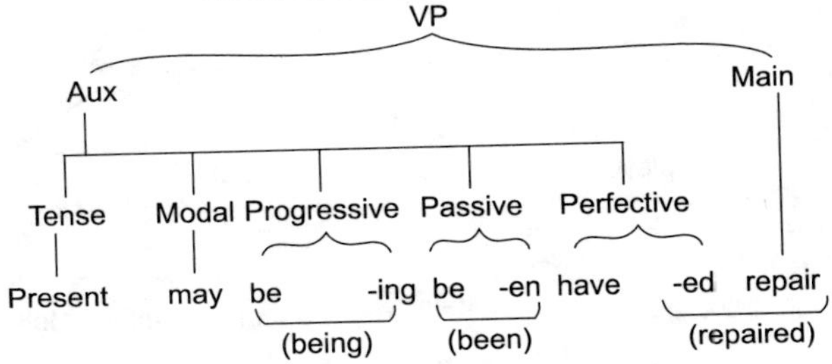

(9) John would have gone.

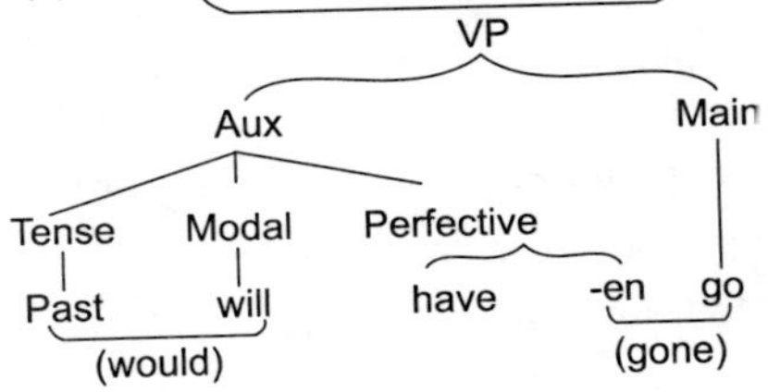

Thus, we see that each component of a VP adds to the characteristics of a sentence.

Apart from these two central components—'auxiliary and main' of a VP, there are other phrases like adjective phrases, adverb phrases, prepositional phrases and noun phrases as well which may remain attached to verb phrases. All of these will be discussed under the heading phrase structure rule of this chapter.

8.2.2 Clausal Constituents (clauses as parts) of Sentences

Simple sentences are joined to make multiple sentences. These multiple sentences (traditionally called compound and complex sentences) are produced as a result of three processes —coordination, subordination and embedding. We know that coordination produces compound sentences, and subordination and embedding produce complex sentences. Look at these one by one.

(I) The constituents of a multiple sentence produced by coordination—

'Ali played and Salah slept.'

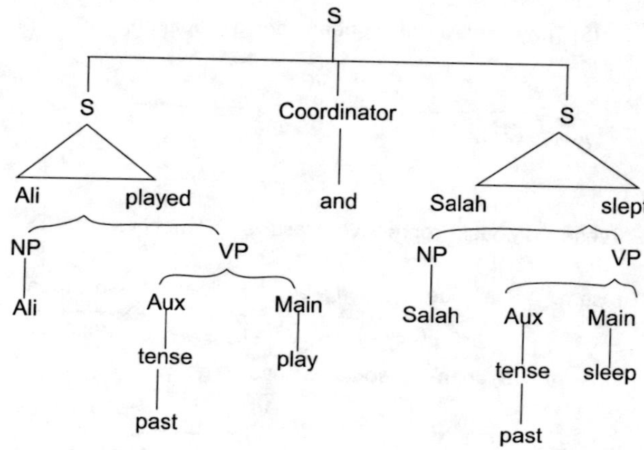

(II) The constituents of a multiple sentence produced by subordination—

'They went while it was raining'.

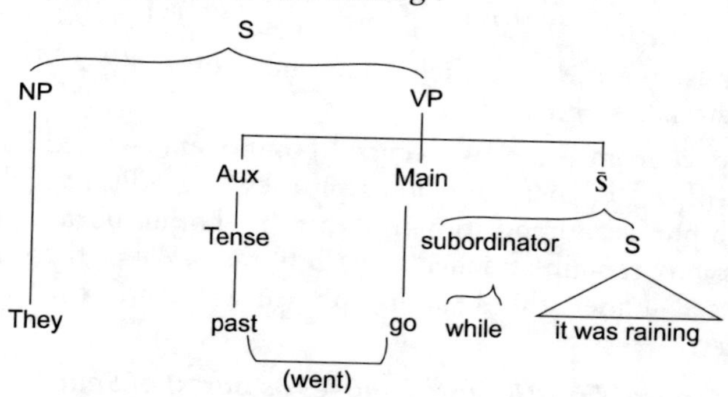

[S̄ = subordinator + s]

Here, 'S̄' stands for subordinate clause that has a subordinator and the attached clausal component (it was raining) as its constituent. Since these clausal components exist almost like sentences, we use 's' as a node to represent them.

Moreover, it is relevant to make clear that the process of subordination takes place when a clause occurs as an adjunct, that is an optional element of a sentence. An adjunct is one of the functional categories that give additional information like adverbs in a sentence. In the sentence given above, the subordinate clause is an adjunct that makes it a case of subordination. This clause gives additional information in this sentence as its meaning will remain unaffected even after the removal of this subordinate clause.

(III) The constituents of a multiple sentence produced by embedding—

'They found that situation was bad'.

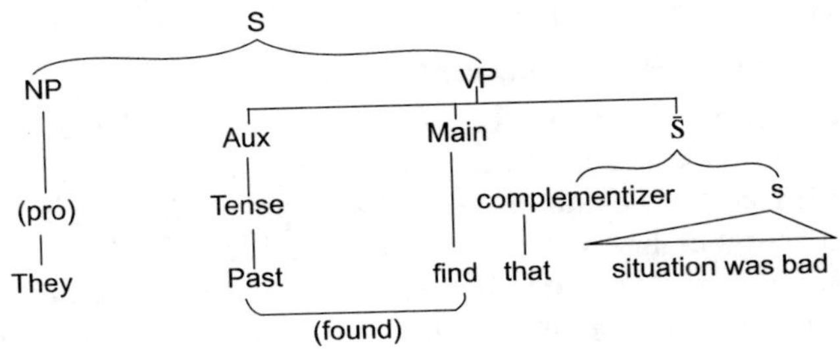

[S̄ = complementiser + s]

When a clause of a sentence constitutes the nuclear element (subject, object, complement) in terms of functional categories of that sentence, the process involved in the formation of this multiple sentence is called embedding. The constituents of such sentences are generally shown through complementizers as given above. In the sentence given above, the clause 'that situation was bad' must not be treated as a subordinate clause because without it the meaning of the sentence can't be obtained. Such clause is called embedded clause as it functions as one of the nuclear elements in this sentence. Since such clauses complete the meaning of a sentence, they need complementizers.

8.3 Some Theories of Syntactic Analysis

A scientific analysis of sentence has been one of the chief concerns of linguistics right from the beginning. Actually, this task of analyzing a sentence into its constituents in a scientific manner is really very challenging. What happens is that our highly imaginative mind produces a variety of sentences under the diverse contexts. These contexts are created due to the complex nature of the real life situations. To give expression to such complexities of life, our mind explores all kinds of possibilities into which the constituents of a sentence may be presented. This results into a very wide range of expression, and hence, it becomes extremely challenging to accommodate all these expressions under the particular sets of rules. Because of this, we haven't been successful in evolving an absolutely scientific theory of sentence analysis till date. But some of the theories have largely succeeded in presenting a convincing analysis of sentences. Let us look at some of these theories.

8.3.1 Immediate Constituent (IC) Analysis

The concept of the 'Immediate Constituent' was brought by Bloomfield, the noted structural linguist of the 1st half of the 20th century. This analysis attempts to establish the fact that a sentence has several constituents identifiable at different levels, i.e. at the level of phrase, words and morphemes. In this analysis, a sentence is divided into two parts, the natural semantic units. Again each part is divided into two parts, and the same process is followed down to the level of morphemes. The structure that is divided is called constitute and the two products of its division are called immediate constituents. Look at this sentence.

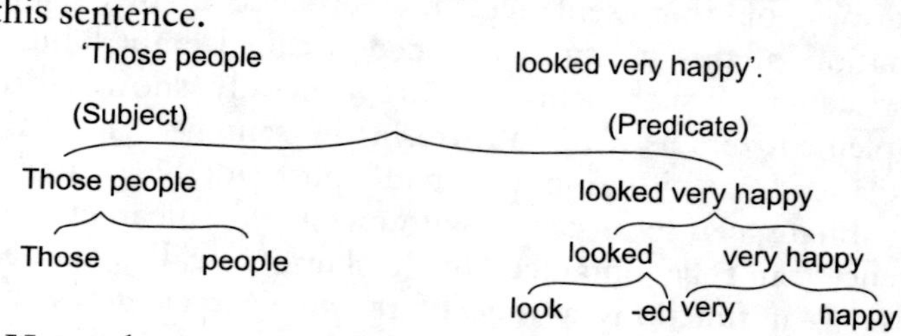

Here the two natural semantic units are subject and predicate. By the term natural semantic unit, we mean the two meaningful parts of a sentence that come to our mind at first reading. The whole sentence is constitute, and 'Those people' and 'looked very happy' are its immediate constituents. These immediate constituents become constitute for successive (following) divisions and the process continues up to the minimal grammatical level that is morpheme.

To a certain extent, this analysis gives a clear picture of the constituents of a sentence. But it fails to analyze those sentences which are ambiguous such as—'time flies'. It has got two meanings as both the words can be used as 'noun' and 'verb' giving two meanings. Because of the lack of labelling at subsequent stages, the IC analysis fails to deal with such sentences satisfactorily. Moreover, sometimes it becomes impractical to divide a particular semantic group into only two parts, e.g. the group 'his brothers, sisters and parents' cannot be convincingly divided into two immediate constituents. Thus, this IC analysis has some serious limitations as a theory. Later on, the comprehensive approach of phrase structure theory overshadowed its importance. In spite of this, the significance of the IC analysis as a valuable chain in the history of sentence analysis will always be acknowledged.

8.3.2 Phrase Structure Rule

It is that rule which tells us about the linear and vertical relationship among the different phrasal constituents of a sentence. This rule considers a sentence to be made up of two immediate constituents—noun phrase (NP) and verb phrase (VP). According to this rule, the first layer of structure for any sentence is NP and VP. Here we assume that an NP may be made up of one word (either noun or pronoun) or a group of words. Likewise, a VP may have one word or a group of words. Then they are further divided into their subsequent components leading down to the single lexical (word) unit. It can better be understood with the help of this sentence.

Those boys were playing.

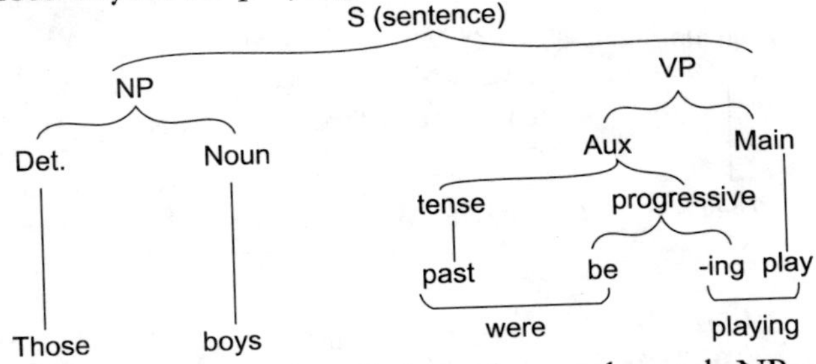

In this structure 's' is called mother node, and, NP and VP are called daughter nodes. Again this NP is mother node for 'determiner' and 'noun'. Likewise, VP is the mother node for 'aux' and 'main'. The point is that the source node that produces the subsequent nodes becomes mother nodes in the channel. Mother nodes are also called dominant nodes, and, daughter nodes are called dominated nodes. The last node where we get individual words (the lexical items) is called terminal node. For the sentence given above—those, boys, play, etc. are all terminal nodes as the classification comes to an end here. The relationship between mother and daughter node is vertical or hierarchical, whereas the relationship between two daughter nodes NP and VP which are also called sister nodes, is linear. Thus, the vertical relationship between 'S' and 'NP' and 'VP', makes these nodes daughter nodes, while linear relationship between NP and VP makes them sister nodes.

The phrase structure rule (P – S rule) for the sentence given above is written like this.

S → NP – VP

NP → Det – N

VP → Aux – Main

Aux → Tense

Let us consider some sentences for phrase structure rule.

(1) They have sold those books.

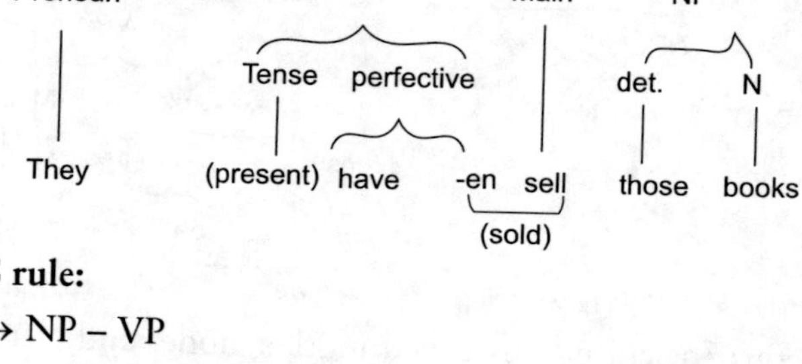

P-S rule:

S → NP – VP

NP → (Det) – N (pro)

VP → Aux –Main – NP

Aux → Tense – Perfective

Here, 'det' has been kept in bracket to indicate that in one of the two NPs of this sentence, it is present as an optional element. If any phrase appears at two or more places in the structure of the P-S rule, it should be represented in one string only. In the above mentioned structure NP appears twice, that is as sister node of VP and daughter node of VP. But in P-S rule, it gets one string only that describes the features of both the NPs.

(2) The students were reading in the class.

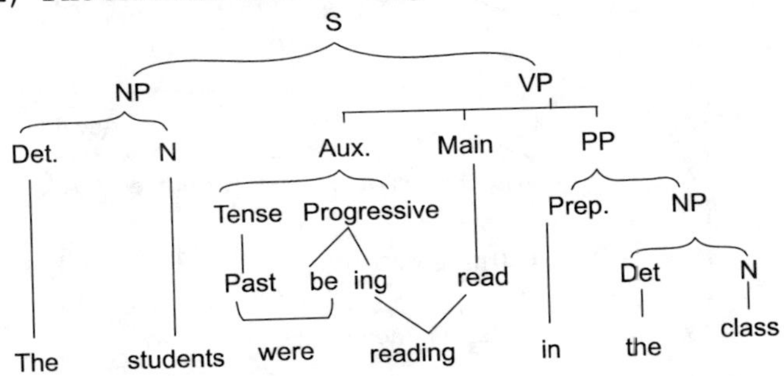

P-S rule:

S → NP – VP

NP → Det. – N

VP → Aux – Main – PP (prepositional phrase)

PP → Prep – NP

Aux → Tense – Progressive

(3) The teacher gave a book to his student.

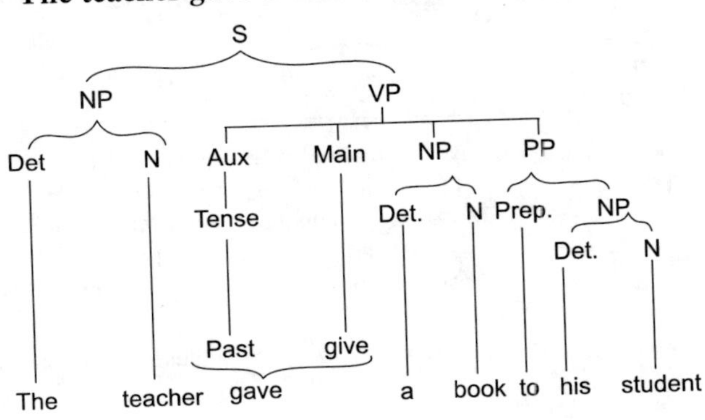

P-S rule:

S → NP – VP

NP → Det – N

VP → Aux – Main – NP – PP

PP → Prep – NP

Aux → Tense

(4) They have done this work very well.

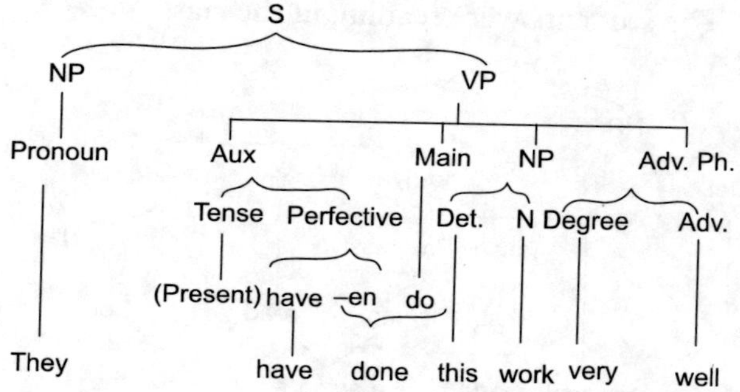

P-S rule:

S → NP – VP

NP → Det – N

VP → Aux – Main – NP – Adv. Ph.

Aux → Tense – Perfective

Adv. Ph. → Degree – Adv.

(5) Flowers look very beautiful in the morning.

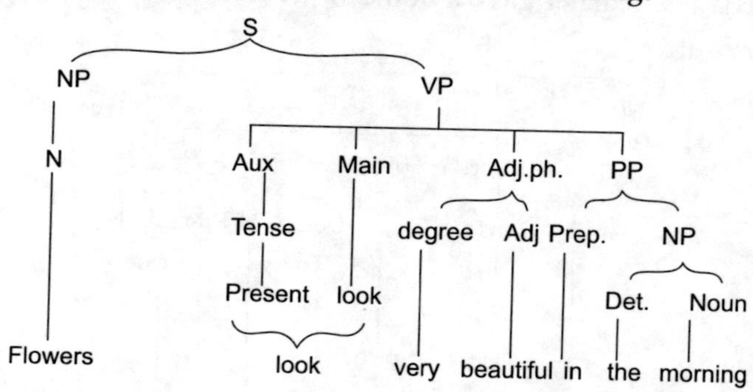

P-S rule:

S → NP – VP

NP → Det – N

VP → Aux – Main – adj. ph. – PP

Aux → Tense

Adj. ph. → Degree – Adj.

PP → Prep. – NP

Through these examples, it becomes clear that different phrasal components like adverb phrase, adjective phrase, prepositional phrase, etc. of a sentence can be shown through two immediate nodes NP and VP of 'S' node. This phrase structure rule gives a very convincing picture of different layers of structures working within a sentence.

Although the P-S rule showed a considerable improvement upon the IC analysis in many ways, it has some serious limitations. It fails to account for the semantic aspects of sentences. For example, the structure like 'Ali plays football' and 'football plays Ali' will have the same analytical structure which indicates the lack of semantic consideration of this rule. Further, it does not give satisfactory explanation of the constituents of complex sentences. The ambiguities of sentences like—'flying planes can be dangerous', 'visiting professors can be costly', etc. cannot be eliminated through this rule. Therefore, an attempt has been made through transformational generative grammar to overcome these inadequacies of phase structure rule.

8.3.3 Transformational Generative Grammar

The concept of transformational generative grammar (TG grammar) was brought by Noam Chomsky, a well-known linguist of the second half of the 20th century, in his book *Syntactic Structure* published in 1957. Considering the fact that phrase structure grammar works in the case of the simple sentences only, and it fails to give a satisfactory analysis for all kinds of sentences, Chomsky came out with the concept of TG grammar. The main objective of the TG grammar is to provide a scientific analysis for all kinds of grammatical sentences produced in a language through certain finite sets of rules. This grammar works on two basic theories of transformation and generation of sentences, and tries to evolve a scientific procedure for satisfactory description of syntactic structures produced in a language.

8.3.3.1 The Concept of transformational generative

When we look at different kinds of sentences produced in a language, it is realized that all the complex structures are derived from simple structures through the act of permutation or combination. That is to say, complex sentences or varieties of sentences are obtained as a result of transformation of the simple sentences. Chomsky talks of deep structure and surface structure of sentences in this regard. He considers the simple sentences which are explained by P-S rule as deep structures, and those structures which are derived from these deep structures are called surface structures. For example, the deep structure—'They play chess' may produce the surface structures like these.

(I) Do they play chess?

(II) Do they not play chess?

(III) Chess is played by them.

(IV) Chess is not played by them.

(V) Is chess played by them?

(VI) Is chess not played by them?

(VII) What do they play?

Thus, it can be seen that one deep structure may produce many surface structures through the process of transformation.

This deep structure is kernel sentence and surface structures are transforms. All these transforms can be explained with the help of kernel sentence by the application of the rules of transformation. To clarify it further, a sentence like —'They came but went away very soon' is transformation of two sentences—'they came' and 'they went away very soon'.

Thus, this concept of transformation brought about a large number of sentences of a language under the range of scientific analysis.

As regards the concept of generative, we can look at it in such a way. Any finite set of rules should account for all kinds of grammatical sentences that may be produced in a language. The kernel sentence is the source and the rules of transformation are the agents, and both of these working together, generate all kinds of possible structures. The term generative has been employed in this sense. That means surface structures are generated by deep structures through the application of transformational rules. Therefore this concept has been named Transformational-Generative. Of late, Chomsky considers generative grammar as that which is rigorous and explicit in description because of the approach it adopts in order to characterize the structures of sentences in different languages.

8.3.3.2 Transformational rules

The kernel structures are simple, assertive, declarative or active sentences that may easily be analyzed according to phrase structure rule. But the surface structures are complex, interrogative, negative, passive sentences, etc. Therefore, certain rules are applied to derive the surface structure from the deep structure, and it adds to the descriptive adequacy of such sentences, i.e. the surface structures can be better understood in the light of these rules. Let us look at some of these rules.

Rule 1. Interrogative Rule: The application of this rule produces an interrogative sentence (surface structure) as a result of derivation from a kernel sentence (deep structure). This rule can be shown in the following way.

Deep Structure			**Surface Structure**	
NP + Aux.	+ Main	→	Aux. + NP + Main	
Tense, modal, be, have, -ed/-en, -ing			tense, modal, be, have	-en, -ed, -ing

Here, we find that in addition to the change in place of main categories like NP and Auxiliary, affixes (tense, -ed/-en, -ing) also change their places. Without change of the place of these affixes, the derivation of surface structure is not possible. Therefore, one of the transformational rules is related to switching of these affixes which is called affix switch rule.

Rule 2. Affix Switch Rule: During the representation of phrase structure of a kernel sentence, we have seen that 'tense', '-ed/-en' and '-ing' work as affixes under the heading 'Auxiliary' as they need a base to be attached to. These affixes are placed before the main verb in the phrase structure tree. For the derivation of the surface structure from the deep structure, the place of these affixes is changed. These affixes are shown attached to the respective bases in order to realize the surface structure. It can be shown like this

Tense, modal, be, + Main →	Modal, be +	Main
have, -en/ed,	have,	-en/ed
-ing	tense	-ing

Let us see the application of these rules through some examples.

(a) 'Have they gone?' is a surface structure in interrogative form. According to transformational rules, it has been derived from the deep structure—'They have gone'. The phrase structure of this deep structure is shown like this.

D.S. → They – (present) – have –en –go.

Interrogative → (present) – Have –they –en –go.

Affix switch → Have (present) –they –gone.

(b) Are they going?

D.S. → They – (present) –be –ing –go.

Interrogative → (present) –be –they –ing –go.

Affix switch → Be – (present) –they –going.

(are)

Rule 3. Do -support Rule: This rule is applied in those cases where auxiliary "do" is required to make an interrogative sentence. For example, the surface structure—'Do they walk?' has been derived from the deep structure—'They walk'. Further, 'tense' as an affix comes before NP in an interrogative sentence and it cannot be attached with NP as it is a constituent of verb only. Therefore, 'do' is supplied as a base with which 'tense' is affixed in order to realize the surface structure. Look at the analysis.

D.S. → They – (present) – walk.

Interrogative → (present) –they –walk.

Do support → (present) –do –they –walk.

Affix switch → Do – (present) –they –walk.

Here, we find that in interrogative structure, present tense cannot be attached to 'they' the NP as 'tense' is an integral part of verb only. The problem is solved by the introduction of 'do' and the interrogative sentence (surface structure) is obtained.

Rule 4. Wh-substitution and Wh-fronting Rules: These rules are applied in the derivation of interrogative sentences starting with wh-words like why, what, where, etc. These rules are called so because the place of wh-words is changed in order to realize the derived surface structure. Look at these examples.

(a) Surface Structure—Where have they gone?

Deep Structure—They have gone somewhere (where).

D.S. → they–(present)–have –en –go –somewhere.

Wh-substitution → they – (present) –have –en –go –where.

Interrogative → (present) –have –they –en –go –where.

Wh-fronting → Where –(present) –have –they –en –go.

Affix switch → Where –have –(present) –they –gone.

(b) Surface Structure—Why are you shouting?

Deep Structure—You are shouting for something (why?).

D.S. → You –(present) –be –ing –shout –for –something.

Wh-substitution → You –(present) –be –ing –shout –why.

Interrogative → (present) –be –you –ing –shout –why.

Wh-fronting → why –(present) –be –you –ing –shout.

Affix switch → why –be –(present) –you –shouting.
(are)

Here we see that wh-words are used as substitutes and then they are brought to the front for the realization of surface structures.

Rule 5. Passivisation Rule: The application of this rule produces passive sentences as surface structures from deep structures. This rule can be seen as follows.

Deep structure Surface structure

NP1+	Aux+	Main+	NP2	-	NP2+	Aux+	Main+	By+	NP1
	Tense					Tense	-ed/en		
	Modal					Modal			
	Be, have					Be, have			
	-ed/en					Been			
	-ing					being			

Examples

(a) Deep Structure—They have eaten bananas.

Surface Structure—Bananas have been eaten by them.

D.S. → They –(present) –have –en –eat –bananas.

Passive → Bananas –(present) –have –been –en –eat –by –them.

Affix switch → Bananas –have –(present) –been –eaten by them.

(b) Deep Structure—Ali will play football.

Surface Structure—Football will be played by Ali.

D.S. → Ali –will –(present) –play –football.

Passive → Football –(present) –will –be –ed –play by Ali.

Affix switch → Football –will –(present) –be –played by Ali.

Rule 6. Negative Rule: Negative sentences are derived as surface structures from the deep structures following the rule given below.

Deep Structure			Surface Structure			
NP +	Aux Tense Modal Be, have, -ing, -ed/-en	+ Main –	NP +	Aux Tense Modal Be, have	+ Not +	Main -ed, -en, -ing

Examples

(a) Deep Structure—You have gone.
Surface Structure—You have not gone.
D.S. → You –(present) –have –en –go.
Neg. → You –(present) –have –not –en –go.
Affix switch → You –have –(present) –not –gone.

(b) Deep Structure—He was eating.
Surface Structure—He was not eating.
D.S. → He –(past) –be –ing –eat.
Neg. → He –(past) –be –not –ing –eat.
Affix switch → He –be –(past) –not –eating.
was

Now let us look at some miscellaneous examples.

(I) Deep Structure—That boy played chess.
Surface Structure—Did that boy play chess?
D.S. → That boy –(past) –play –chess.
Interrogative → (past) –that boy –play –chess.
Do -support → (past) –do –that boy –play –chess.
Affix → Do –(past) –that boy –play –chess.
Did

(II) Deep Structure—He has broken the chair.

Surface Structure—The chair has been broken by him.

D.S. → He –(present) –has –en –break –the chair.

Passive → the chair –(present) –has –been –en –break –by –him.

Affix switch → the chair –has –(present) –been –broken –by –him.

(III) Deep Structure—He reads poems.

Surface Structure—What does he read?

D.S. → He –(present) –read –poems.

Wh –substitution → He –(present) –read –what.

Interrogative → (Present) –he –read –what.

Wh -fronting → what –(present) –he –read.

Do-support → what –(present) –do –he –read.

Affix switch → what –do –(present) –he –read.

(IV) Deep Structure—You learnt English.

Surface Structure—What did you learn?

D.S. → You –(past) –learn –English.

Wh -subs → You –(past) –learn –what.

Interrogative → (past) –you –learn –what.

Wh -front → what –(past) –you –learn.

Do-support → what –(past) –do –you –learn.

Affix switch → what –do –(past) –you –learn.

did

(V) Deep Structure—They will win.

Surface Structure—They will not win.

D.S. → They –(present) –will –win.

Negative → They –(present) –will –not –win.

Affix switch → They –will –(present) –not –win.

Thus, it is seen that among all these rules, affix switch rule comes at last that produces the desired surface structure in all the cases. These rules truly show the mechanism involved in realization of surface structures from deep structures, and thereby, help us in developing an insight into the syntactic intricacies of sentences.

The distinctive features of TG grammar may be summarized as follows.

(I) It attempts to evolve certain finite sets of rules that may account for infinite number of grammatical sentences produced in a language.

(II) It has immensely succeeded in disambiguating many complexities related to syntactic structure.

(III) It has contributed to the degree of scientificity, explicitness, grammaticality and descriptive adequacy of sentences.

(IV) It strikes at the inner mechanism of working of a language at intuitive level, and explores the possibility of accountability for the linguistic creativity of users.

(V) It is very comprehensive and almost all inclusive in its approach as it strives to include in its fold all aspects of sentences.

Though TG grammar has remarkably succeeded in exploring new dimensions in the sphere of syntax, it has its own limitations. Its pioneer Chomsky has made several modifications in his theories since it started in 1957. From this point of view, it is still not complete as the modifications are going on. These modifications have made TG grammar a complex bundle of rules, not easy to understand. Despite these reservations, TG grammar can certainly be acknowledged as a very significant achievement in the domain of syntactic analysis.

Exercises

Q1. What is syntax? How is it different from morphology?

Q2. What do you mean by the constituents of a sentence? What are these constituents?

Q3. What are the constituents of a noun phrase?

Q4. What are the constituents of a verb phrase? Draw a tree-diagram showing these constituents.

Q5. What is phrase structure rule? What are its specific features?

Q6. What do you mean by immediate constituent analysis? Give its example.

Q7. What are the limitations of the phrase structure rule?

Q8. What is transformational generative grammar? Does it give a more convincing analysis of a sentence than that of the phrase structure rule?

Q9. Mention the important transformational rules?

Q10. What are the important features of transformational generative grammar?

Q11. Show your acquaintance with the following terms.

(a) Determiner (b) Modifier
(c) Quantifier (d) Classifier
(e) Kernel sentence (f) Complementiser

Q12. Bring out the differences between these terms.

(a) Pre-determiner and post-determiner
(b) Pre-modifier and post-modifier
(c) Deep structure and surface structure
(d) Time and tense
(e) Subordination and embedding

Q13. Analyze the different parts of these noun phrases and name them.

(a) Most of those good singers
(b) An ill-built house in Ranchi.
(c) The most interesting Greek plays
(d) All the first five novels of Dickens
(e) Some of the very bright English students of Arts' college

(see the answers after the last chapter)

Q14. Draw the tree-diagrams of the phrase structure for the following sentences. Write down the P-S rules also for them.

(a) Abdullah runs a shop.

(b) That boy is working hard.
(c) The best student has topped in the examination.
(d) Those students may have gone for a picnic.
(e) My friend is very short.
(f) The teacher said that the earth is round.
(g) He was playing and I was reading.
(h) I came when it was raining.
(i) He may have been being rewarded.
(j) Those people will be leaving tomorrow.

(see the answers after the last chapter)

Q15. Write down the surface structures for the following deep structures of sentences.

(a) Ali opens the door.
(b) They like novels.
(c) You are very intelligent.
(d) We went there.
(e) He will come soon.

Chomsky's Universal Grammar

9

9.1 What is Universal Grammar (UG)?

Noam Chomsky, as the proponent of cognitivism in the second half of the 20th century, brought forth some novel ideas about the knowledge of language that revolutionized the whole corpus of linguistic studies. He proposed that all the human beings are endowed with innate language learning capacity. Our brain has a separate language faculty that is equipped with the grammar of all the human languages. The existence of this universal grammatical system located in the language faculty with potential to account for all the linguistic operations taking place in human languages is termed as UG. Depending on the response from the society in which we grow and use language, the grammar of that language gets activated. This external linguistic stimulus, that is technically called triggering experience, picks up that grammar which accounts for the sentences used in this language. This proposition is principally based on the observation that the properties of individual languages are extractions from a broad set that contains all the linguistic properties together in one whole. Each language of the world contains some of these properties with the help of which it functions. This broad whole consisting of all the linguistic properties exists as something hardwired in the language faculty of human brain. The exposure to the linguistic items of an individual language provides the natural stimulus for the learners which helps them in picking up the items of their mother tongue very fast as the rules governing this language already exist in their brain. The concept of UG is based on this principle. Chomsky, thus, considers UG as a system of principles, conditions and rules that are elements or properties of all the human languages.

9.2 The Basis of UG Theory

The advent of UG theory invoked a serious debate among the linguists who construed it as an extreme view. Hence, Chomsky provides a logical basis to his UG theory through the introduction of cross-linguistic data or evidences along with reliable laboratory operations. He says that a child uses sentences which he/she never hears. Technically, it is called poverty of the stimulus argument. A child produces unheard sentences only because of the subjection of the input (items of the mother tongue) to some mental operations, i.e. this input stimulates the hardwired linguistic apparatus, that is also called Language Acquisition Device (LAD), which processes it leading to the new kind of output (unheard sentences). This processing becomes possible only due to the innate linguistic endowment. Chomsky considers language faculty as a faculty independent of all other faculties of brain that contains the exclusive software for individual's linguistic affairs. This language faculty is the seat of UG which has a set of principles and parameters that determine the properties of human languages. He finds these principles as universal properties of languages such as, structure dependency, movement of Noun Phrases, embedding of clauses, etc. whereas parameters as the properties that vary from one language to another (discussed below). These language specific features in the form of principles and parameters are unique to the domain of language faculty which establishes its autonomous identity among all the faculties of human mind. This set of principles and parameters may account for all possible grammatical constructions in all the human languages. Because of this set, a native speaker of a language intuitively understands the acceptable and deviant expressions of this language. Several researches conducted on children with a view to testing their native language ability approved the idea that they easily distinguish between correct and incorrect expressions without having grammatical ability to explain the nuances involved. This also lends credence to the theory of UG.

Further, several researches conducted in medical sciences have shown that some children suffer from certain linguistic disorders like aphasia, dyslexia, etc. which are directly associated with the deformities in the nervous system or genotypic traits. It supports the view of existence of separate language faculty as Chomsky claims. Apart from this, a corpus of research has proved that the growth of language among children takes place at a uniform pace without the role of conscious effort or external factor, i.e. cascade effect. Those children, who are brought up in a multi-lingual environment, pick up more than one language with equal dexterity or on a par with the children growing in monolingual settings. It indicates that the existence of UG facilitates the learning of many languages even at a very early stage. The researches conducted on establishing the relationship between language learning ability and IQ levels have proved that this ability is not directly related to the IQ levels. It has been seen that many children have astonishing language learning capacity despite low IQ and vice versa. Children suffering from 'Specific Language Impairment' show normal cognitive development. This dissociation between intelligence and language learning ability reinforces the biological endowment of UG. Various researches conducted on language learning ability of animals have shown that they cannot learn discrete linguistic items like human beings regardless of the intense effort. Our much developed organs of speech also hint at the biological endowment of language. Moreover, the identification of speech control area inside the brain (Broca's area) supports the view of innateness hypothesis. All of these largely instantiate the relationship between human brain and linguistic manifestation that gives a strong basis to UG theory. Dobzhansky, a biochemist, found out in 1970 that 'each individual's genotype determines the potential range of functional adaptations to the environment'. This may rightly be applicable to the linguistic genotype of human beings that gets reflected as UG. The triggering experience provided by the environment sets the ball rolling resulting into the gradual development of linguistic faculty, the phenotypic manifestation. Much research is underway in neurolinguistics and many findings till date strongly support the Chomskyan view of UG as a reality.

9.3 The Notion of Principles and Parameters

Chomsky's theory of principles and parameters is very significant in the framework of Universal Grammar (UG). This theory suggests that the knowledge of language that is innately endowed among human beings has a set of two kinds of linguistic features separately termed as principles and parameters. Those linguistic features which are common to all the languages, are universal principles, whereas those which vary from one language to another, are called parameters. These principles and parameters constitute the fundamental basis of UG that is accounted for the linguistic competence a child is born with, i.e. UG is present in a child's mind as a system of principles and parameters. The principles are fixed and constant elements marking the universal features of languages, and the parameters are some highly restricted variable elements specific to individual languages. Let us have a look at some of the important principles and parameters observed in natural languages.

Major Principles of UG

9.3.1 Structure Dependency

It is a principle that proposes that all languages are structure dependent, i.e. the change in sequence of phrases that constitute sentences will either alter the meaning or make the sentences ungrammatical. But it does not imply that all the languages have the same grammatical structure. We have "subject + verb + object" in English, whereas "subject + object + verb" in Hindi and Japanese. In order to produce different kinds of sentences in a language, we have a set of rules regarding structures that account for the grammaticality of sentences. Likewise, each language is structure dependent and any deviation from the rule bound structure will produce ungrammatical sentence. Chomsky says—"All known formal operations in the grammar of English, or of any other language, are structure-dependent" (1971).

9.3.2 Headedness Principle

This principle advocates that each phrase has a head word without which a phrase cannot exist. As we have seen earlier in the chapter syntax that a sentence consists of phrases and each phrase has a head word after which this phrase is named. For instance, a noun phrase has a noun as the head word, a prepositional phrase has a preposition as the head word, etc. Look at the sentence 'His son is at the gate' which has 'son' as the head word of noun phrase, and 'at' as the head of the prepositional phrase. Likewise, in Hindi sentence 'uska beta darwaje par hai' 'beta' and 'par' are the head words of noun and prepositional phrases.

9.3.3 Embedding Principle

It is a principle which states that subordinate clauses are embedded in languages in general. Look at these sentences of English and Hindi respectively—'He went when it was raining' and 'Wah gaya jab warsha ho rahi thi'. The cases of embedding are commonly observed in French, Arabic and many Indian languages. This shows embedding as a universal principle which is applicable in natural languages.

9.3.4 Projection Principle

It proposes that the properties of words of a language determine the syntactic features, i.e. the structure of a sentence largely depends on the semantic feature of words used in it. As for instance, a verb like 'give' will take a subject, a direct object, and an indirect object, for producing a grammatical and meaningful sentence. A sentence 'He gave a book to me' contains all the items given above, and so, it is a complete sentence. Look at these incomplete expressions.

He gave me. (what)

He gave a book. (to whom)

He gave. (what)

All of these structures are incomplete syntactically as well as semantically that is because of the semantic property of the word 'give'. Likewise, there are words like 'prefer' 'buy' 'weep', etc. which have semantic features that condition the structure of sentences accordingly. Such words are found in all the languages. In Hindi, the words like 'peetna' (beat), 'dena' (give), 'kharidana' (buy), etc. have semantic features which determine the structure of sentences.

Maine use peeta. (I beat him)

Usne mujhe ek kitab dee. (He gave a book to me)

Usne ek kitab kharidee. (He bought a book)

These examples clearly show that the structures of these sentences are conditioned by the semantic features of the verbs used in them. All the words given above have semantic projections that need to be accommodated in syntactic frames permissible in a language.

9.3.5 Locality Principle

This principle states that grammatical operations are usually local in nature, i.e. these operations take place among the words which are physically close to each other in a sentence. An English sentence like—'He has been living in Delhi for ten years' has 'has been' as auxiliary verb. When it is changed into an interrogative sentence, 'has' is fronted, not 'been'. We say—'Has he been living in Delhi for ten years'? We don't say 'Been he has living in Delhi for ten years'? It shows that the auxiliary that is close to the subject is fronted conforming to the locality principle. Likewise in Hindi, a sentence like—'Ram bhat aur Sita roti kha rahi thi' (Ram was eating rice and Sita was eating bread), the verbal ending (feminine) is controlled by the subject (Sita) that is closer to the verb. It approves the locality principle.

Major Parameters of UG

9.3.6 Head Parameter

All the phrases that constitute a sentence have head words like noun for noun phrase, verb for verb phrase, preposition for prepositional phrase, etc. These head words have complements either before or after them varying across languages. For example, in English, these complements appear after the head words and so, it is considered as head first language. Look at these constructions.

> the book on the table ('on the table' complement of Noun)
>
> prefer syntax ('syntax' complement of Verb)
>
> in college ('college' complement of Preposition)

All these examples show that English is a head first language because heads appear before the complements. But Hindi is a language in which heads come after complements in expressions like—table par (on the table), kamare me (in the room), Aman ka ghar (house of Aman). So, Hindi is a head last language. On this basis, it is generalized that a language can be either head first or head last. This is called head parameter as it varies from one language to another unlike principles.

9.3.7 Pro-drop Parameter

There are some languages in which pronouns used as subjects are dropped in declarative sentences and a sentence starts with a finite verb. Languages like Arabic, Italian, Chinese, etc. have such structures. Since this phenomenon is language specific, it is a parameter. In Arabic, we say—yathadath alogalarabia (He speaks English). In this expression of Arabic, there is no pronoun equivalent of 'he' of English. It is different in English/Hindi where a pronoun used as a subject of a formal sentence can't be dropped. We can't say—'Am a teacher' in the place of 'I am a teacher'. Likewise in Hindi, we can't say—'ek shikshak hun' in the place of 'main ek shikshak hun'.

On the basis of the examples cited above, we can easily understand the difference between principles and parameters. Moreover, the principles are different from the traditional concept of rules in the sense that a rule is specific to a particular kind of construction of a language, whereas a principle is applicable to the constructions across the languages. The principles are the broadest constructs that subsume rules. Chomsky says—"The basic assumption of the Principle and Parametre model is that languages have no rules at all in anything like the traditional sense, and no grammatical constructions (relative clauses, passives, etc.) except as taxonomic artifacts" (1995). He does not view a language as a set of rules rather as a set of specifications in terms of parameters evolved in the light of the invariant principles. As for instance, the structure dependency is a principle that provides a broad framework inside which the system of language specific parametric variations like 's+v+o' or 's+o+v', etc. are introduced.

9.4 UG and Language Acquisition

The process of language acquisition holds a very significant place in the framework of UG. Actually, Chomsky's concept of UG derives its sustenance from some concrete observations and findings drawn from the domain of language acquisition only. The theory of UG foregrounds the process of language acquisition through which Chomsky convincingly extends his arguments of innate endowment. As per the conventions of UG, the language faculty of a child has a computational system along with principles and parameters that interacts with the input (external stimulus), i.e. the linguistic item of the mother tongue, and transforms it into something quite new (unheard sentences). Apart from this, there is space for lexicons that get activated with the listening of words of the mother tongue. When a child starts getting exposure to the items of his/her mother tongue, the computational system of the UG gets activated and starts acting upon this external stimulus. It gradually sets the parameters for this mother tongue as they vary across languages, whereas principles contained in this mother tongue stand in tune with invariant universal principles already existing there in the language faculty. Further, Chomsky talks of 'fixed principles governing possible sound systems' and 'a rich and invariant conceptual system' as the contents of UG that may reasonably be considered as parts of the universal principles (1988). All of these principles and parametres work in coordination in the course of interaction with the external stimulus which results into the creation of a core grammar of the mother tongue that helps a child produce grammatical sentences.

Here, acquiring a language, thus, means setting the values for all the parameters such as, for English, head first, non-pro-drop, etc. and for Hindi, head last, non-pro-drop, etc. which we have already seen earlier in this chapter. The vocabulary items are acquired with the help of principles governing sound systems that deal with pronunciation, and projection principles that introduce syntactic restrictions depending on the properties of words. Likewise, the different aspects of the mother tongue are taken care of by different kinds of principles and parameters resulting into its complete acquisition. At this stage of acquisition, a child develops the grammatical competence (core grammar) that is fully determined by the governing principles, parameters and vocabulary items that account for the properties of his/her mother tongue. But it doesn't mean that all aspects of a language are fully covered by UG. For instance, in English, irregular verbs, concepts of plurality in certain words (sheep, cattle, man), etc. are the aspects which go unaccounted by UG. Chomsky defends it by bringing forth the concept of core and periphery grammar, in which, the core accounts for all the features covered by UG, whereas periphery accounts for those which are not covered by it. Therefore, the acquisition or learning of such irregular verbs of English appears to be challenging for native children as well as the non-native adult learners who learn it as a second/foreign language. Since the domain of language is very vast, UG can't be held responsible for non-inclusion of such peripheral aspects of languages which can be seen as gradual additions to linguistic repertoire resulting from sociolinguistic interactions.

Thus, we see that UG provides a logical account of language acquisition. The linguistic competence of a child consists of the activation of the principles, setting of the parameters and creation of the core grammar. This competence enables the native speakers of a language to make distinction between grammatical and deviant structures intuitively. The goal of linguists working in Chomskyan tradition, who are called generativists, is to enquire about the nature of this intuitive linguistic competence. They are entrusted with the task of bringing out theories regarding language acquisition in different languages which may determine the principles of UG along with parametric variation in the language in question on the basis of the input (linguistic items) and creation of the core grammar as a result of interaction among these components. A theory that clearly outlines all such aspects of a language is supposed to have attained explanatory adequacy according to Chomsky.

9.5. Some Major Theories of UG

Since UG intends to encapsulate the universal attributes of languages and tries to formulate theories that may account for the linguistic operations in all the human languages, Chomsky has evolved certain theories in the frame-work of principles and parameters that help us understand the universal grammatical features from a different perspective. He suggests that different theories working within the domain of principles and parameters, are involved in the construction of sentences, and each theory may be independent of others, which is technically known as modular approach. Here, each theory is regarded as a separate module and a sentence is viewed as a product of complex networking of these modules. Now, let us have a look at these theories.

9.5.1 X-bar Theory

This theory deals with the phrasal structure/constituents of sentences in human languages. The theory claims that each sentence of a language is a combination of phrases (Noun phrase, Verb phrase, Adjective phrase, Prepositional phrase) which have head words belonging to the same lexical categories, i.e. a noun will be the head word of an NP, a verb will be the head word of a VP, and so on. We have seen the representation of phrasal constituents in English sentences in the chapter 'syntax' where all the constituents of a phrase have been shown at the same level. Let us have a look at that.

(a) A book on the table (NP)

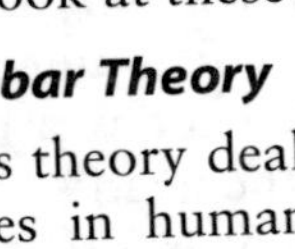

(b) Bought a book from a shop (VP)

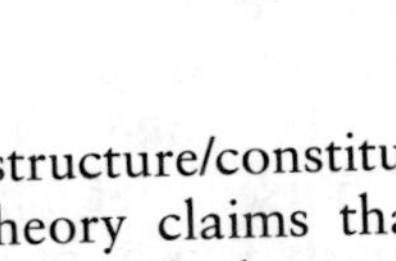

Both of these examples show that all the constituents of NP and VP have been kept at the same level as they are all sister nodes. This representation doesn't show the hierarchical relationship among the sister nodes due to which we cannot understand the degree of closeness existing among these constituents. For example, in 'a' the relationship between 'det' and 'N' is not the same as is the relationship between 'N' and 'PP'. Likewise, in 'b' the relationship between 'Verb' and 'NP' is different from the relationship that exists between 'V' and 'PP'. The above representation fails to capture such differences in the relationship of the different constituents which is considered as an inadequacy. The X-bar theory proposes a hierarchical structure of phrases that introduces an intermediate level which clearly shows the relationship among the constituents, and adds to the explanatory adequacy of sentences across the languages in the framework of principles and parameters theory.

Chomsky says 'Phrases typically consist of a head and an array of complements determined by the lexical properties of the head' (1986). The implication is that a head stands in a very close relationship with that phrase which functions as its complement compared to other phrases which function like adjunct. To make it more clear, a complement is a complete phrase in itself that makes the meaning of the head complete in terms of its lexical projection. A complement in this sense can be an object (NP), a prepositional phrase, etc. depending on the requirement of lexical projection. An adjunct, on the other hand, gives extra information in a sentence and does not remain strongly bound to the head like complements. According to Chomsky, an X-bar structure is composed of projections of heads selected from the lexicon (1993). He talks

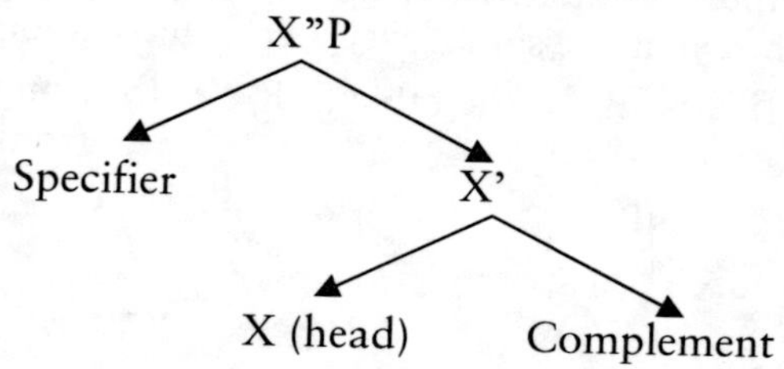

of maximal projection shown as—X" (with double bar), intermediate projection shown as—X' (with single bar), and minimal projection shown as—X (without a bar). The structure of a phrase in the scheme of X-bar theory appears as follows.

This structure is the basic frame of X-bar structure through which the different elements of a phrase are represented. Here, X stands for any lexical phrase like noun, verb, adjective, Preposition. A specifier comes in the place of determiner which is a functional category as this structure takes into account functional categories except the head for which lexical category is used. A specifier is that word which precedes the head of its containing phrase. Determiners are specifiers as they appear before the head words of the phrase of which they are parts. The specifiers are much inclusive and so, it becomes convenient to present distinctive features of phrases with their help. The X' is the intermediate level which is the sister node of 'specifier'. A complement is the sister node of the head (lexical category). Since this structure includes lexical (formal) as well as functional categories into account, it is called cross categorial representation of phrases as the head represents the lexical category (noun, verb, adjective, preposition) and other items represent functional categories (complement, specifier, adjunct). In this structure, an adjunct appears as the sister node of X', the intermediate level if it is a part of the phrase. Let us see some examples.

(a) 'very mad after cricket'

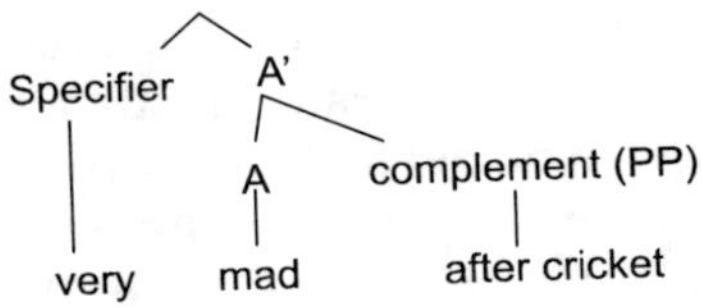

Phrase structure rule—

Adj P—Specifier; A'

A'—A; complement

(b) 'a book of English'

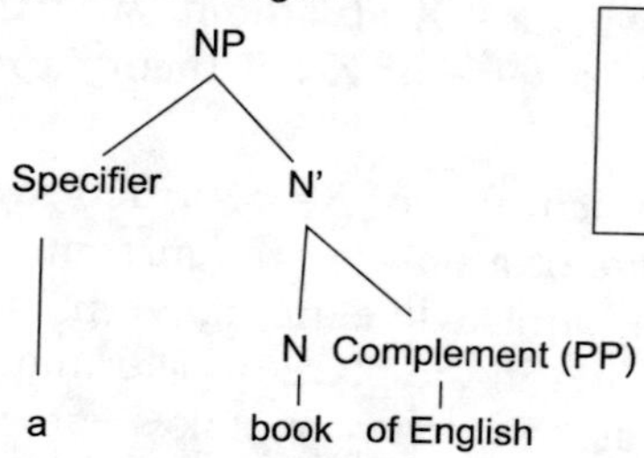

Phrase structure rule—

Np—specifier; N'

N'—N; complement

(c) 'read a novel in the class'

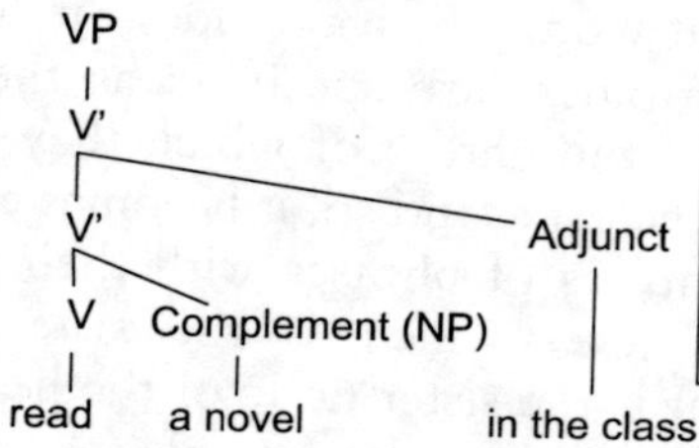

Phrase structure rule—

VP—(specifire); V'

V'-V'; adjunct

V'-V; complement

Thus, we see that X-bar structure clearly shows the hierarchical relationship existing among the constituents of various phrases. It is very clear from the given diagrams that a complement is the sister node of the head, whereas an adjunct is the sister node of single bar level above the head. It represents the degree of relationship between the head, its complement and adjunct which was a major inadequacy of the flat tree diagrams in which all of these constituents were represented at the same level.

In terms of phrase structure rules, X-bar theory does not propose any order of occurrence between the constituents, i.e. a complement may come before a head or after a head depending on the nature of a language. Since English is a head first language as we have seen earlier, the head comes before the complement. In Hindi, a phrase like—'Sudhir ki kitab' (Sudhir's book) will be represented as follows.

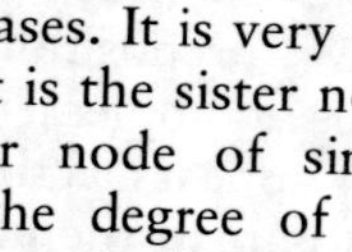

Phrase structure rule—

NP – N'; specifier

N' – N; complement

Here, we see that the head is preceded by the complement reflecting head last feature. Thus, X-bar theory attempts to capture the universal feature of hierarchical structure of phrases in human languages as a principle and gives space for the accommodation of parametric variation across them conforming to the principles and parameters theory.

9.5.2 Theta (Θ) Theory

This theory proposes a systematic explanation of the lexical projections of grammatical entities that determine the syntactic features of a sentence across the languages in the framework of principles and parameter theory. It states that the semantic range of grammatical entities like verbs, prepositions, adjectives, etc. play a very important role in the construction of a sentence. Let us look at some sentences:

(a) Ram sent a letter to his father.

(b) She wrote a book.

(c) I smile usually.

We see that lexical features of the verbs in all of these sentences determine the structure of these sentences, i.e. 'send' needs a sender, something (letter) to send, and a receiver. Thus, a sentence with 'send' as the main verb will be complete and acceptable only if it has got all the constituents given above. Likewise, we find that 'write' as a verb needs a writer and a product (book) that is written. A verb like 'smile' needs someone to do the act of smiling. These are the minimum requirements of such verbs to produce a meaningful sentence. All such grammatical entities that largely determine the structure of a sentence are technically called predicates. This concept of predicate is not to be confused with the traditional concept of predicate of a simple sentence. A verb like 'send' thus, is a three place predicate as it essentially needs three elements, a verb like 'write' is a two place predicate that needs two essential elements, and a verb like 'smile' is a one place predicate as it needs one essential element. All these essential elements are called the arguments of their predicates, i.e. the verb 'send' has three arguments and likewise the case with 'write' that has two arguments, and 'smile' has one argument.

These arguments are the referring entities realized as persons, things, etc. and can rightly be considered as parts of lexical projections of the predicates.

The theta theory advocates that a predicate assigns certain roles to its arguments which are called thematic roles. These thematic roles are identified as an agent (doer of an action), a patient (receiver of an action), a theme (thing affected by an action), a goal (beneficiary of an action), etc. For instance, in sentence 'a' given above 'Ram' is the agent (subject argument), 'letter' is the theme (NP argument), and 'his father' is the goal (NP argument). In sentence 'b' 'she' is the agent (subject argument), and 'book' is the theme (NP argument). In sentence 'c', there is only one agent that is subject argument. All of these arguments emanate from the lexical properties of their respective predicates. As regards the relationship between arguments and theta roles, each argument of a predicate is assigned one theta role, and each theta role is assigned to only one argument. This is called theta criterion. A sentence can be a grammatical construction only if this criterion is fulfilled. Let us see a sentence with an adjectival predicate.

He is jealous of me.

In this sentence, the adjective predicate 'jealous' has two arguments 'he' and 'of me' because someone has to practise jealousy, and for this act to be practised, a stimulant (me) is required. These two arguments assign two theta roles (each argument one theta role), 'he' as the agent and 'of me' as the theme. This fulfils the theta criterion and the sentence becomes complete as an expression like 'he is jealous' cannot be considered complete unless the cause of jealousy is given, i.e. jealous of what. In the examples discussed above, we see that a predicate has arguments to its left (before the predicate) and right (after the predicate), if there are two arguments of it as is the case with 'jealous'. In this case, 'he' is considered as external argument (subject argument), and 'of me' as internal argument (complement argument). In English language, the position of these two kinds of arguments is to the left and right of the predicate, i.e. subject argument appears to the left and complement argument appears to the right. Now, let us look at these Hindi sentences.

Usne ek kitab likhee (He wrote a book).

Maine use peeta (I beat him).

In the first sentence, the subject argument for the verbal predicate 'likhee' is 'usne' and the complement argument is 'ek kitab'. This subject argument is assigned the theta role of agent, and complement argument is assigned the theta role of theme. Likewise, in the second sentence, the subject argument is 'maine' for the verbal predicate 'peeta', and the complement argument is 'use'. These two arguments assign the theta roles of agent and patient to 'maine' and 'use' respectively. Thus, the theta criterion is fulfilled in both the sentences. Further, we see that both the arguments appear to the left of the predicate, subject argument is followed by the complement argument. This feature which varies across languages is captured by parametric variations.

9.5.3 Government and Case Theory

The theory of government talks about the relationship among different constituents of a sentence basically in terms of governor and governed. We see that certain features of some constituents of a sentence restrict the choice of some other constituents in the same sentence. The constituents that impose such restrictions are governors, and the constituents that are realized as resultant forms of such impositions, are governed. This relationship between governor and governed can be understood in a better way with the illustrations of grammatical cases in sentences.

In English sentences, the object of a verb is realized in accusative case, while its subject is realized in nominative case. Look at the sentence—'He called me' in which the case features of 'he' (nominative case) and 'me' (accusative case) are determined by the verb 'call'. Hence, this verb is the governor, and its subject and object are governed. This verbal constituent restricts the choice of grammatical case, as we cannot use 'him' or 'I' in the place of 'he' and 'me' respectively. Likewise, a preposition governs its object as its accusative form can only occur after it. In a sentence like—'They talked about me' we cannot use 'I' in the place of 'me'. A preposition, thus, restricts the choice of case of its object. So, this preposition is a governor, and its object is governed.

The case theory in the frame of UG proposes that in any sentence some constituents are case assigners and some are the receivers of cases. For example, verbs and prepositions are case assigners as they assign accusative cases to their objects as we saw in the examples given above. We have already seen in the previous chapters that tense is an integral part of a finite verb and it conditions the choice of a subject. So, it is assumed that this tense assigns nominative cases to subjects, whereas the lexical verb assigns accusative case to its object in English sentences. There is physical proximity between the constituents in case assignment, i.e. the assigner and the assigned are immediate constituents, as a tense assigns case to its immediate left (subject position), and a verb assigns case to its immediate right (object position). A preposition occurs just before its object. Government and Case theory is part of universal principles found across the languages. The diversity observed in the direction of case assignment and the physical proximity among the constituents of sentences of a language is subject to parametric variation. Look at these sentences of Hindi.

'Unlogaon ne use mara' (They hit him).

'Wah mere sath gaya' (He went with me).

Here, 'unlogaon' has nominative case and 'use' has accusative case. Both of these words are assigned cases from the finite verb that has tense as an integral part. The lexical verb 'marana' assigns accusative case to its object 'use', and its past tense assigns nominative case to the subject 'unlogaon'. Thus, the case assigners are governors that determine the cases of subject and object like English sentences. Further, the preposition 'sath' assigns accusative case to its object 'mere', and the tense of intransitive verb assigns nominative case to the subject. It is relevant to mention that an intransitive lexical verb does not assign case as it has no object. So, a preposition is a governor that assigns accusative case to its object.

In both of these sentences, we find that the proximity as well as the direction between the assigner and the assigned is different from what we found in English. Because of the structural difference between Hindi and English sentences, here, tense assigns nominative case to the subjects but they are not immediately left to the tense. Further, the verb, in the first sentence, assigns objective case to its object which is to its left unlike English where the object comes immediately after the verb. Moreover, preposition in Hindi is preceded by its object unlike English where the object of a preposition succeeds it. These differences are accommodated under the heading parametric variations in the frame of UG.

9.5.4 Binding Theory

This theory deals with the relationship existing between noun phrases and some forms of pronouns like reflexives (himself, myself), reciprocals (each other, one another), and pronominals (him, them), in a sentence. The term 'binding' implies syntactic and semantic bonds of such pronouns with noun phrases they refer to. Technically, reflexives and reciprocals are also called anaphors as they refer to specific nouns in a sentence, and such nouns are known as antecedents. The nouns or pronouns which occupy the subject positions are called referring expressions. Let us look at these sentences.

(a) They praise themselves.

(b) We like each other.

(c) Pratyush beats him.

In the first sentence, 'themselves' refers to 'they'; in the second sentence, 'each other' refers to 'we'; but in the third sentence, 'him' does not refer to 'Pratyush'. The pronominal 'him' refers to an entity outside the domain of the given sentence. The binding theory attempts to explore the dimension of such relationships in a sentence with an eye to the grammaticality involved in the framework of UG. The anaphors and their antecedents are co-indexed that is represented with the symbol (i) in a sentence. Now consider these sentences.

Ram said that his friend killed himself.

I like my students to study themselves.

Here, 'himself' refers to 'his friend' not to Ram, and 'themselves' refers to 'my students' not to 'I'. It establishes that the concept of binding operates in a local domain, i.e. the anaphors and the antecedents exist within the same clause as is the case in the given sentences. On the basis of these observations, it is deduced under the heading binding theory that—

(a) Anaphors are bound as they refer to their antecedents in a sentence.

(b) Pronominals are free as they refer to the entity outside the domain of the sentence.

(c) Antecedents or referring expressions are also free like pronominals.

Let us see its implications in Hindi. Look at these sentences.

(a) Ramesh apni prashansa karata hai (Ramesh praises himself).

(b) Ramesh uski prashansa karata hai (Ramesh praises him).

(c) Ramesh ne kaha ki uska dost apni prashansa karata hai (Ramesh said that his friend praises himself).

In the first sentence, 'apni' is anaphor with Ramesh as its antecedent. In the second sentence, 'uski' is the pronominal referring to an entity outside the domain of the sentence. In the third sentence, 'apni' refers to 'uska dost' not to Ramesh, which indicates the operation taking place in a local domain, i.e. inside a clause, as we saw in the case of English sentences. It shows that this theory is applicable across the languages. Certain structural differences in sentences of different languages may be explained in terms of parametric variations.

Thus, we see that all these theories mentioned above corroborate to the concept of UG, as they are applicable across the languages. Each of these theories is independent of others but they interweave a pattern that accounts for almost all the grammatical operations with the help of which a language works. For instance, the implications of theta theory, projection principles, case theory, etc., are always there in the production of a grammatical structure but there is ample scope of autonomy with which each one of these theories can be looked into. This view justifies the modular approach adopted to interpret linguistic phenomena under the framework of UG.

9.6 Minimalism: The Latest Innovation

Chomsky has been modifying his theories of UG since the inception of cognitivism. After having realized the complexities, and to some extent, inadequacies of the principles and parameter theory in interpretation and analysis of the true nature of language, he shifted his focus towards economy and precision in presentation and derivation of universal features of languages under the concept 'minimalism'. He lays emphasis on phonetic and semantic components of language in minimalism and considers them to be sufficient to account for various linguistic phenomena. Chomsky puts it like "Each language can be regarded as a particular relationship between sound and meaning" (1972). Any language basically operates with sound-meaning interface. We listen to sounds of a language that are transformed into meanings by certain mental operations making the act of communication possible. The physical realization of the phonetic component of a language undergoes a computational system inside the mind that changes these signals into meanings, the semantic component of a language. The response of mind to the phonetic component is governed by sensorymotor system, whereas its transformation into semantic component is governed by conceptual-intentional system. Both of these systems work at the point of interface, i.e. at the point of interaction of PF and LF with the computational system. The sensorymotor system responds to the external stimulus (sound) and modifies it according to the requirement of the computational system for further processing. The conceptual-intentional system integrates the modified linguistic input with the object (concrete) or idea (abstract) that this input intends to refer. This process can be seen in this figure.

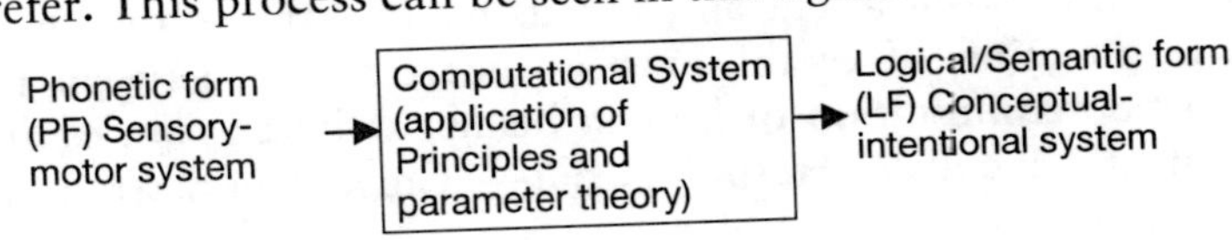

The semantic form is realized in a logical form as meaning is derived based on logic with the application of syntactic rules in computational system. Actually, syntax plays a very vital role inside the computational system. For instance, look at the sentence 'That boy is intelligent'. Here, the sounds of the words that appear in a sequence are interpreted in terms of syntactic rules operational inside the computational system resulting into the logical derivation of the meaning. Because of this, the semantic component represents a logical form. This logical form represents that partial meaning which is determined by the syntactic structure. This meaning undergoes contextual interpretation leading to the final semantic component. The syntactic structure plays a central mediating role between the physical form (phonetic component) and abstract meaning (semantic component). This computational system applies the theories of principles and parameters, such as structure dependency, projection principles, theta theory, etc. on the input, i.e. phonetic component. This application transforms the phonetic data into meaningful units.

As regards the system of computation, Chomsky talks of mental lexicon. Each individual has a set of lexical entries (words) inside the mental faculty that contains lexical properties of these items as well. These lexical items realized in phonetic form are subjected to syntactic operations that take into account their projection properties. For instance, a word like 'help' has to be tested in terms of its lexical projection, that is to say, whether it has a subject and an object. This word 'help' needs someone as a helper and someone to be helped as we have already seen in projection principles. The computational system sets the order of the words depending on the information it has about these words in the mental lexicon. The sequence of words so evolved becomes an acceptable grammatical structure leading to a logical meaning.

Chomsky's emphasis on mental lexicon in minimalism as a concept draws our attention towards his relentless effort made in the direction of establishing a concrete link between the linguistic manifestation of human beings as living entities and our mental faculties. He points out—"Current understanding falls well short of laying the basis for the unification of the sciences of the brain and higher mental faculties, language among them" (2005). Much research is underway in the area of mental lexicon today which is largely inspired by the Chomskyan ideology. Minimalism as the latest theoretical advancement in the tradition of UG, is truly an extension of his previously advocated principles and parameters theory which has been adequately and reasonably accommodated in the computational system of the current theory.

Exercises

Q1. What do you mean by Universal Grammar (UG)?

Q2. How will you substantiate the existence of UG?

Q3. How are the principles different from the parameters in UG framework?

Q4. Write notes on the followings.

(a) structure dependency

(b) headedness principle

(c) projection principle

(d) head parameter

(e) pro-drop parameter

Q5. Describe the process of language acquisition among children in the framework of UG.

Q6. What is X-bar theory? How does it address the inadequacy of conventional phrase structure analysis?

Q7. What is theta theory?

Q8. Describe the process of case assignment in government theory of UG.

Q9. Introduce the binding theory of UG.

Q10. Present a brief sketch of minimalism.

Semantics

10

10.1 What is Semantics?

Semantics is that field of study in which we talk about the meaning of the words and sentences. It is a fact that meaning is central to any linguistic activity, as wherever we use language, it is meant to convey a kind of meaning only, and so, semantics deals with this fundamental aspect of language. It explores the relationship between a word in the form of sign and the meaning that this sign refers to.

A minute observation of the mechanism involved in the operation of a language makes it clear that words are physical entities that manifest the conceptualizations of worldly experiences (both concrete and abstract) of the members of a particular society that has a common language. That is to say, the concrete objects as well as the abstractions prevalent in the domain of a society are conceptualized and consequently encapsulated in the form of words, and these words are used to transfer the idea (the product of the conceptualization), associated with them in communication. Any language functions on the basis of this precept.

Here, the worldly experiences include physical as well as metaphysical entities, i.e. whatever comes under the purview of imagination of human mind. It can further be understood with this illustration.

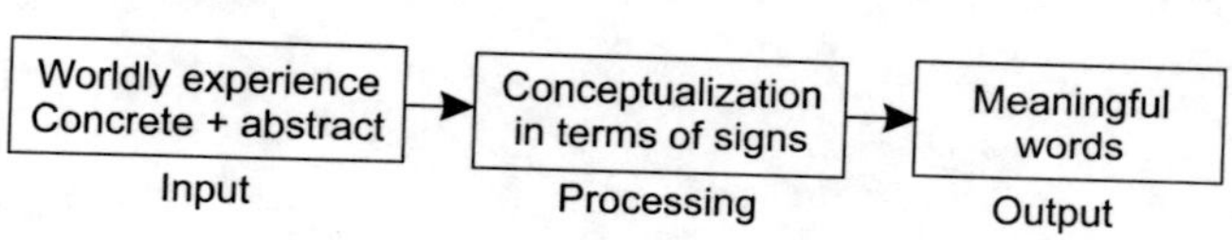

Apart from this, semantics takes into account all the factors ranging from socio-cultural and psychological to grammatical that explicitly or implicitly affect the realization of meanings of the words and sentences. How the meaning of a word or a sentence changes with the change of context, how many kinds of meanings can be derived from a word or a sentence in varying contexts, and how the change of place of a word in a sentence changes its meaning, all these aspects are thoroughly examined under semantics. Let us look at these sentences given below.

A fan gives air.

She is my fan.

He has fanned all the controversies.

A close look at these sentences makes it amply clear that the change of context changes the meaning of a word. The meaning of the word 'fan' is different in each of these sentences, and even each sentence can be explained in terms of more than one meaning. All such issues constitute the realm of semantics. Thus, semantics attempts to analyze and explain the dimension of meaning in a very comprehensive manner. This analytical study of meaning undertaken in semantics proves to be of immense help in developing an insight into the functioning of a language.

10.2 The Meaning of Meaning

The term meaning of meaning initially causes a puzzling effect on us but a sensitive look into it makes the sense clear. This is the uniqueness of studying meaning as the core aspect of language. Meaning can be defined as that totality of impression in terms of worldly experiences, which is loaded or encoded in a word with the objective of transmitting it in order to make communication through language successful. By the term totality of impression, we mean all possible ideas associated with a word. If a word contains more than one meaning, the mutual understanding between the writer and the reader, or the speaker and the listener, helps them in the realization of the intended meaning depending on the context.

The most important aspect in deciding the meaning of a word or sentence is the context in which it is used. Here, the context means the setting, the atmosphere in which the language is used. Look at these sentences.

(1) The king said, "I will wipe the tears of my people".

(2) The mother said, "I will wipe the tears of my crying child".

The meaning of the word 'tear' is different in these sentences because of difference in context. In the first sentence, its meaning is connotative that is implied, and in the second, its meaning is denotative that is direct. In the first sentence tear refers to grief, whereas in the second one it refers to the liquid which comes out of our eyes during weeping. Because of the complex nature of life, human society encounters heterogeneous kinds of situations that create diverse contexts. These contexts create the conducive situation for the widening of the semantic range of a word. The semantic range indicates the range of meaning a word occupies, such as the word 'women' means a human, adult, female, etc.

The world of meaning has been an interesting area of enquiry for a long time. We have been trying to establish a logical connection between a word and its meaning, but this attempt has not been successful till date. What we can say about meaning with certainty is that it is the sum total of a slice of worldly experiences in the form of idea, associated with a word on the basis of mutual agreement among the users of a common language. It is because of this mutual agreement that we communicate successfully as the member of a particular society. This sense of mutual agreement helps us conceive the meaning of a word uniformly among all the users of a language. We have already looked at it in terms of signifier (word) and signified (idea) in the fourth chapter that is also useful in illustration of the concept of meaning.

10.3 Some Concepts of Semantics

As semantics deals with meaning in a very comprehensive and analytical manner, it comes out with many subtle distinctions among closely related terms. An understanding of such distinctions is very crucial to realize the dimension of meaning. Let us look at these concepts.

10.3.1 Semantics and Pragmatics

Semantics, in general, takes into account the meanings of words and sentences in all possible dimensions as stated earlier and so, its field is very extensive. Pragmatics is that field in which we talk about all the possible meanings of a sentence or utterance in a specific context. To clarify it further, how a particular context widens the scope of meaning of a linguistic item (sentence/utterance) becomes the subject matter of pragmatics. Look at these sentences.

(1) Driver, start your taxi.

(2) You come and sit with me, please.

(3) The principal announced the cancellation of all the classes.

In all of these sentences, we find that there is sense (meaning) along with a force of action. The speech leads to an action automatically, and this phenomenon is called speech act. The force associated with these speeches is called illocutionary force that leads to performance of action. The driver starts the taxi, the hearer comes and sits with the speaker, and the classes stand cancelled as a result of the announcement by the principal—all these actions take place as a part of the meaning of the speeches. That means a speech does not convey only meaning rather it initiates an action also in certain contexts. All these meaningful aspects of a linguistic item are studied under the heading pragmatics. Further pragmatics considers the extra-linguistic meanings also, of utterances. For example, when a man orders his servant to bring sugar from shop, he answers "It's raining". Here, the meaning of such an utterance (it is raining) has to be understood in terms of worldly knowledge and experiences, as the servant cannot go out due to rain and so, he cannot follow the order. The meaning is extra-linguistic here in the sense that the literal meaning of the words used in this utterance does not correspond to the expected answer unless it is correlated with worldly knowledge that during rain it is usually difficult to go out. Thus, pragmatics attempts to analyze the meanings of utterances in the light of specific contexts as shown above.

As regards the inter-relationship between semantics and pragmatics, it can be said that pragmatics emerged out of semantics. Though many linguists look at these as two entirely distinct entities, it is difficult to draw a sharp line of demarcation between them. The approach of looking at pragmatics as an off-shoot of semantics seems reasonable in the sense that pragmatics too, explores the new dimensions of meaning under certain specific contexts that may be accommodated under the broad expanse of general contexts. Pragmatics has undoubtedly widened the horizon of semantics to bring to its fold many new concepts like speech act, illocutionary force, performative meanings, etc.

10.3.2 Sentence, Utterance and Proposition

A sentence is a group of words which are arranged according to grammatical rules to produce a complete meaning. It is basically the longest meaningful grammatical unit of a language that begins with a capital letter and ends with a full stop. A sentence has at least a subject and a verb as its constituents.

An utterance is the spoken form of a language. What comes out as speech that contains meaning like sentences is an utterance. An utterance is different from a sentence in the sense that an utterance may be of one word like yes, no, go, etc. that gives complete meaning in a particular context unlike a sentence that must have at least a subject and a verb. Secondly, an utterance is exclusively an oral product, whereas a sentence is usually realized in written forms. Thirdly, an utterance may be explained in terms of pitch, frequency, tone, etc., whereas a sentence may not be. Fourthly, a word or a phrase or a clause may work as an utterance independently but they will not work as a sentence. Look at this piece of conversation.

Ali — What is your name?

Ahmed — Ahmed.

Ali — Where do you work?

Ahmed — In a cement factory.

Ali — What works do you do there?

Ahmed — As my boss orders.

Ali — Do you work there at night?

Ahmed — No.

All the questions of Ali are in the form of sentences, whereas the answers given by Ahmed are in the form of utterances.

A proposition is a semantic unit of a language. Here, the idea expressed in a sentence is considered as unit. A proposition is different from a sentence in the sense that two sentences may have the same proposition. The sentences—'I write books' and 'Books are written by me' have the same proposition as both of these contain the same idea. Further, the change of place of a word in a sentence produces a new sentence but it does not produce a new proposition if the meaning does not change as a result of this change in sequence of words. Look at the sentences—'Two days back he left' and 'He left two days back'. Here, there are two different sentences because of difference in sequence of words, but the proposition is the same as meaning does not change.

10.3.3 Text and Discourse

A text is a piece of writing that is marked by the unity of theme. By the term 'unity of theme' we mean its reading must give a coherent idea about any subject/topic. A text usually consists of sentences and these sentences show a considerable degree of coherence to produce a unified meaning. A text is the largest unit of linguistic activity as it happens to be an end product in itself. A paragraph, an essay or any piece of writing dealing with a particular theme constitutes a text. A good text is characterized by coherence, cohesion, correctness, clarity, etc. Coherence is required for the thematic or semantic unity of text; cohesion gives logical growth to the sentences of a text; correctness of grammar and diction (choice of words) adds to the clarity of meaning. All these contribute to the beauty of a text. To clarify the concept of coherence and cohesion, look at these sentences.

(i) His style of teaching English is very good.

(ii) He studied in England.

Here, these two sentences show coherence because at the level of meaning we can correlate the two sentences. The first sentence is the effect and the second sentence is the cause. Since the teacher himself studied in England (the motherland of English), his style of teaching English became very good. But these sentences do not show cohesion, as no separate linguistic device has been used to connect them. To make these sentences cohesive, the second sentence should have been written like this.

'It is so because he studied in England that is the motherland of English'.

This makes the difference between the coherent and cohesive nature of a text. We use subordinating and coordinating conjunctions like because, although, but, therefore, etc. as cohesive devices in a text.

As regards discourse, it is that linguistic activity which deals with different kinds of interpretations of a text. We know that a text contains message that is encoded by the writer as per his own point of view. This message is decoded by the reader who may get a meaning from this text different from what the writer (encoder) may have intended. This difference in meaning may occur due to the creation of a different context by the reader (decoder). Any literary piece such as, a poem, a prose, a novel, etc. may be interpreted in more than one way that constitutes the subject matter of a discourse. Actually, a word gives more than one meaning in different contexts, and so, it produces primarily the scope for discourse. A text like—'He wants to visit the bank' may produce two discourses because of the difference in the meaning of the word 'bank'—a financial institution, and a side of a river. Thus a text is encoder-centric, whereas a discourse is decoder-centric linguistic activity.

10.3.4 Reference and Sense

Reference and sense are the two ways of realizing the meanings of words. When a word refers to an object or anything that can be seen such as, elephant, book, table, house, etc. its meaning is realized in terms of reference. The word 'elephant' brings to our mind the image of a huge animal that exists in nature. The word 'elephant' is referent and the concept conveyed by this word is reference.

On the other hand, sense is primarily related to those words which do not refer to any object of nature that can be visualized. The words like love, hatred, but, intelligence, etc. do not refer to any object. The meanings of such words are expressed with the help of words conveying the same meaning (synonyms) or opposite meaning (antonyms), etc. For example, the meaning of the word 'love' can be expressed as deep emotional attachment, attraction, affection (synonyms) or opposite of hatred, repulsion (antonyms), etc. Thus we can say that reference is associated with visualization, whereas sense is associated with realization. Reference involves language (word) and the outer world (objects) for its realization, and so, it is supra-lingual, whereas sense is realized through the elements (words/sentences) of language only, and so, it is intra-lingual. Reference expresses the meaning of a word in terms of the objects of nature, whereas sense expresses the meaning of a word in terms of other words of the same language.

10.3.5 Denotation and Connotation

These are the two kinds of meanings of words. Denotative meaning directly refers to that concept for which a word literally stands in a language. For example, the word 'mother' literally refers to an adult woman who has children. Likewise, the term 'lion' literally refers to an adult male animal found in forests. These words (mother, lion) basically exist in English language to convey the above given concepts. It is this denotative meaning which gives a particular kind of identity to an idea or an object in terms of which it is distinctly conceptualized from rest of the ideas or objects existing in the universe.

As regards connotative meaning, it refers to that special idea or concept which is associated with a word in terms of its meaning in addition to its denotative meaning. For example, the word 'mother' in special contexts means affection, devotion, loyalty, etc. Likewise, the word 'lion' stands for courage, aggression, ferocity, etc. These meanings are in addition to the denotative meanings of the words. Such meanings are considered as connotative. The connotative meanings are usually culture specific or species specific, and hence, changeable. For example, in some creatures, mothers feed on their own children, and so, in that particular creature connotative meaning (affection, devotion, loyalty) of the term 'mother' will not be applicable. Thus denotative meaning is literal, uniform, static and objective, compared to connotative meaning that is figurative, culture-specific, changeable and subjective.

10.3.6 Entailment and Presupposition

When the meaning of a particular sentence works as the source of another meaning that can be established in the light of meaning of the first sentence, the process is called entailment. Look at these sentences.

(i) Ali eats rice.

(ii) Rice may be eaten.

Here the meaning of sentence (i) is the source of the meaning of sentence (ii). We can establish that rice may be eaten because Ali eats it. The first sentence entails the second sentence that is a logical extension of the first one and is considered as an entailment.

Presupposition, on the other hand, is a kind of meaning that can be presumed to be correct in the light of the meaning of a given sentence. For example, the sentence 'Ahmed has a beautiful wife' presupposes that Ahmed is married. Thus, presupposition involves the knowledge of the worldly affairs as we know that a man may have a wife only after marriage. Moreover, the worldly knowledge produces a presupposition and a given sentence works only as a frame of reference for it, while an entailment is a derivation fully dependant on the fact of a given sentence.

10.4 Semantic Classification of Words

We have already seen by now that a word may express more than one meaning depending on the context. Further, there are words that give similar meanings. In some cases, the meaning of one word is realized in terms of the meaning of another word that gives exactly an opposite meaning. Based on these criteria, we classify words in terms of the relationship of their meanings. Let us look at these classes of words.

(1) **Synonyms**—It is that class of words which have the similar meaning. This similarity of meaning may not be necessarily found in all the possible contexts. If two words may be used in at least one context inter-changeably, i.e. one word may replace the other without affecting the meaning, they are called synonyms.

The following sets of words are synonyms.

(a) child, baby, kid (nouns)
(b) good, fine, nice (adjectives)
(c) look, see, watch (verbs)
(d) gradually, slowly, steadily (adverbs)

(2) **Antonyms**—It is that class of words which have opposite meaning. These antonyms are broadly classified as gradable and non-gradable (binary). The gradable antonyms refer to those entities which are realized in more than one state, i.e. the concept of degree is applicable to them. For example, the antonyms 'big and small' may be realized as bigger, biggest, and smaller, smallest. The gradable antonyms show the feature of variation in terms of degree.

On the other hand, non-gradable antonyms refer to those entities that cannot exist in more than one form in a matter of fact way. For example, the antonyms 'alive and dead' cannot be graded like—more alive or more dead in real terms. It means one can either be alive or dead, no condition in between exists. The following sets of antonyms will make the idea more clear.

Gradable antonyms	**Non-gradable antonyms**
hot – cold	bachelor – married
dear – cheap	true – false
long – short	male – female
happy – sad	natural – artificial

These examples make it clear that in gradable antonyms, we find intermediary states (middle states) of the things, i.e. if something is not hot, it does not mean that it is cold. It may neither be hot nor cold. But this is not the case with non-gradable antonyms. If someone is not bachelor, it means that he is married. There is nothing in between these two extremes.

(3) **Homonyms**—Those words which are different in meanings but the same in pronunciation and spelling are called homonyms. Look at the word 'bank' which has two different meanings—'financial institution' and 'the side of a river' but in both of the cases its spelling and pronunciation are the same. Hence, they (the word bank used in two contexts) are homonyms. Here are some more examples of homonyms.

Right	/raIt/	Opposite of wrong
Right	/raIt/	Opposite of left
Ring	/rIŋ/	Sound produced
Ring	/rIŋ/	An ornament
Mine	/maIn/	A pronoun
Mine	/maIn/	A source of minerals

(4) **Homophones**—Those words which have different meanings and spellings but are pronounced in the same way are called homophones. Look at these words.

bear --- /beə/	no --- /nəU/	I --- /aI/
bare --- /beə/	know --- /nəU/	eye --- /aI/
right --- /raIt/	sweet --- /swi:t/	hear --- /hIə/
write --- /raIt/	suite --- /swi:t/	here --- /hIə/

(5) **Homographs**—Those words which have different meanings and pronunciations but are spelt (written) in the same way are called homographs. Look at these words

tear	/tIə/	liquid that comes out of eyes
tear	/teə/	to make pieces of something
wind	/wInd/	blowing air
wind	/waInd/	to make twists or bends
lead	/led/	a metal
lead	/li:d/	to guide

These homographs are called heteronyms also by some linguists.

(6) **Polysemy**—When one word is used to refer to more than one meaning, i.e. literal and metaphorical, it is called polysemy. There are many words, the literal meaning of which is extendable up to metaphorical level. For example, the literal meaning of the word 'head' is that organ of our body which controls all other organs. Depending on this literal meaning, this word is used in metaphorical sense to refer to the head of an office/family/party, etc. Here, these two meanings are not entirely different like homonyms rather one meaning is extended up to the other meaning. The expressions like 'arms of a clock', 'needle of suspicion', 'foot of a hill', etc. refer to polysemy of the words arms, needle and foot respectively. Likewise, look at these polysemous words.

mouth	an opening in the body for food intake
mouth	the mouth of the volcano
root	the underground part of a tree
root	the source of anything
leg	the part of our body that helps to stand
leg	the legs of a table/chair

(7) **Hyponyms**—There are some words that represent a broad category of certain things. Under this broad category, small category falls. The relationship between this broad and small category is called hyponymy and the words that represent these two categories are called hyponyms. For example, the word 'furniture' is a big category, and the words 'table', 'chair', 'bench', etc. are small categories of furniture. Thus, the relationship between furniture and all these items 'table', 'chair', 'bench' is that of hyponymy. Look at some other examples of hyponymy.

Flower – rose, jasmine, marrigold, etc.

Literature – novel, play, poetry, etc.

Stationery – pen, paper, pencil, etc.

10.5 Semantic Theories

By the term semantic theories we mean that set of ideas which help us in understanding the true nature and dimension of meaning in a scientific manner. A semantic theory intends to explain and analyze the domain of meaning very comprehensively. The scientific interpretation of meaning has been a serious concern of the linguists for a long time and it has resulted into the emergence of many theories as such with passage of time. Let us look at some of these theories.

10.5.1 Referential Theory

This is one of the oldest theories of meaning. It says that meaning is the relationship between a word and the object that it refers. We know very well that words are used to indicate the different objects found in nature. In the beginning of human civilization, mankind would have realized the need of naming different objects for purposeful communication. In the due course, they may have named different objects depending on the specific socio-cultural and linguistic circumstances prevailing at that time. Even today, when we invent something, we name it immediately for our convenience in communication. In the process of naming it, we try to include its meaning in terms of its function or features. For example, a computer is that electronic device that computes, and so, it has been named according to its function. Likewise, different objects may have been named by our fore-fathers based on the then existing socio-linguistic situation. In terms of explanation of meanings, the semanticists try to establish a link between the term used and the object referred. Here, it is relevant to describe the concept of Ogden and Richards (1921) in this connection.

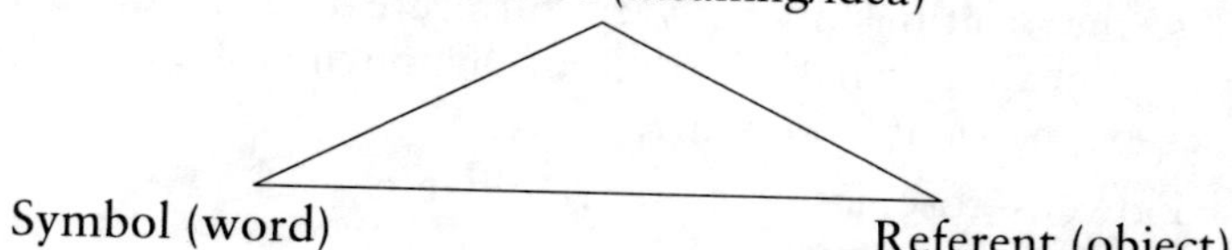

They have tried to explain the relationship among a word, the object referred and the meaning conveyed through this given triangle. They consider a word as a symbol that refers to an object which is considered as referent, and the idea that is conveyed, as reference. This reference contains the meaning which remains operational even in the absence of referent, and communication takes place. Thus this referential theory considers meaning as the relationship between the symbol (word) and the referent (object). But this theory fails to give a concrete explanation in case of sense words that cannot be seen like objects. Apart from this, it has not been possible till date to establish the inherent scientific relationship between a word and the object it refers, and so, the domain of meaning remains unexplained in this theory. In spite of these serious limitations, the referential theory of meaning holds an important place in the channel of semantic theories.

10.5.2 Componential Analysis Theory

The whole universe is a vast network of relationships. This relationship remains operational at several levels. Words are used to express this complex relationship in all the languages. As we have already talked about meaning relations among words, some words represent the bigger categories while some smaller ones in terms of worldly experiences and knowledge. For example, the word 'male' represents a broad category that may further be divided into different life forms like humans, animals, birds, reptiles, etc. Here, all these life-forms can be classified as either male or female. Keeping this vast, complicated network of associations in mind, some semanticists came out with this theory that aims at analyzing the meaning of a word in terms of its bigger categories. This theory talks of a word as a component of a big concept that subsequently happens to be a component of a further bigger unit making a chain of relationships. According to this theory, the meaning of a word is expressed with the help of positive (+) and negative (–) markers. Look at these words and their meanings.

Word	Meaning	Word	Meaning
1. Man	+ human + male + adult	2. Cow	+ animal – male + adult

3. Dog	– human + male +adult	4. Book	+ material + countable – living
5. Boy	+ human + male – adult	6. Water	+ material – countable – living

Here, positive and negative markers indicate quite opposite features. All the examples given above, show that the meaning of a word is expressed in terms of certain big categories to which this word belongs. For example, the term 'human' includes man, woman, child, boy and girl, and so, these terms are treated as components of the bigger category 'human'. Thus, we come across many features that a word encapsulates following this componential analysis theory.

But this theory fails to give a uniform kind of analytical tool for many words. Some words can be described in the ways shown above, particularly the nominal (noun) words, but majority of the words cannot be expressed in terms of such parameters. This is a very serious limitation of this theory.

10.5.3 Contextual Theory

As the name implies, this theory considers the context of situation as the most important factor in describing the meaning of a word or sentence. The term 'context of situation' was firstly used by Firth in 1957. He expressed his view that the meaning of a word is better understood or decided on the basis of its use in a particular context. This context includes linguistic as well as non-linguistic situation. Here, linguistic situation includes phonetic, grammatical or semantic features of a word or a sentence, whereas non-linguistic situation means the worldly knowledge of a speaker or a hearer who uses a language. Look at the following sentences.

(i) The host bought some beautiful cups.

(ii) The host bought some beautiful cups to serve tea.

(iii) The host bought some beautiful cups for the winning teams.

The meaning of the first sentence does not become clear on the basis of the linguistic situation as the words 'host' and 'cup' give two meanings and both of these are applicable in these sentences. Here non-linguistic situations may clarify the meaning. If this sentence has been used in a context of serving tea to the guests or giving prizes to the winning teams, then only its meaning comes out clearly. These two are non-linguistic situations that require worldly knowledge on the part of the speaker or listener, i.e. guests are served tea in cups and winning teams are given cups as prizes. These two obvious meanings have been made clear in the second and third sentences, with the addition of specific linguistic contexts. On the basis of these examples, it can be said that this context or situation is related to discourse as the sentences second and third are the possible discourses of the first sentence. The inter-relationship between context and meaning can be seen through this diagram.

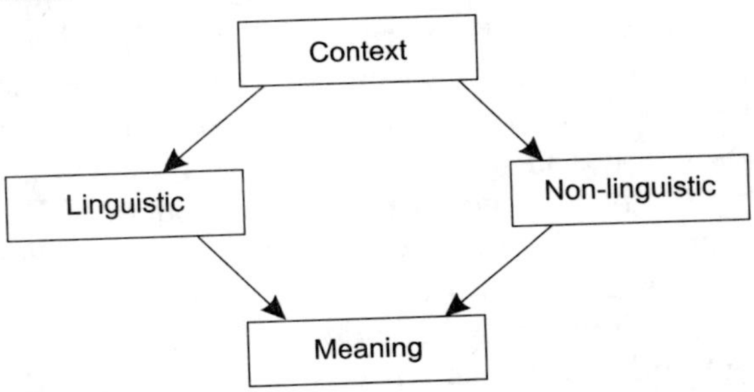

Thus, this theory advocates that any linguistic item (a word or a sentence) acquires meaning in terms of the context of situation. The dimension of meaning is manifested in the varieties of contexts that may be created in real life situations. This theory of meaning is comprehensive as it starts from semantics and goes down to the level of pragmatics. Moreover, it attempts to interpret meaning with a practical approach.

10.5.4 Transformational Generative Theory

This theory is an off-shoot of the Chomskyean concept of T.G. grammar. Here, we look at the semantic implications of syntactic structures presented and described by Chomsky. His concept of deep and surface structure has already been discussed in the chapter syntax. As regards the meaning he says —it is deep structure that determines the meaning features of a sentence. In the light of the meaning of a deep structure, the meaning of surface structures can be interpreted. A very sincere attempt has been made in this theory to correlate the syntactic structure with semantic features. It is a fact that different words are used in a sentence keeping in view their individual meanings and grammatical aspects. That means there must be harmony between meaning and structure to produce a meaningful sentence. Look at these sentences.

(i) Ali plays football.

(ii) Football plays Ali.

Here, the first sentence is correct but the second one is incorrect because of the lack of harmony between meaning and structure. Though, for both of these sentences, the phrase structure rule will be the same. It indicates the importance of meaning feature in the formation of a meaningful sentence. To solve this problem, the concept of 'selection restriction' has been introduced. This concept says that only certain sets of subjects will stand in agreement with certain sets of verbs. In the examples given above in the first sentence 'Ali' the subject is '+ human' which agrees with transitive verb 'play' and so, the sentence is meaningful and correct. In the second sentence 'football' is '– human' which does not agree with transitive verb 'play' and so, the sentence is meaningless and incorrect. The rule of selection restriction talks of harmonious combinations in sentences. In this context, Chomsky gave this popular example—'colourless green ideas sleep furiously' which shows disharmony between semantic feature and syntactic feature resulting into a meaningless sentence. To make it clear further, we cannot say 'The table laughs' because 'laugh' as an intransitive verb will always go with a subject that is '+ –human' not with a '–human' subject like table.

Thus, the theory attempts to look at meaning in relation to the structure of a sentence. The deep structure contains the fundamental meaning that appears in different modified forms in surface structures. The application of transformational rules to deep structure results into modifications of meanings but these modifications can easily be explained in terms of the basic meaning of the deep structure.

Apart from the theories of meaning mentioned above, there are certain theories like stimulus-response theory, operational theory, interpretive theory, etc. which attempt to explain the nature and scope of meaning. All these theories have their own merits and limitations. No theory propounded so far has successfully encapsulated the range and explained the true nature of meaning in an absolutely logical manner. But these theories definitely help us in developing an insight into the realm of meaning. The exploration of semantic world continues to be an interesting sphere of research for the linguists.

Exercises

Q1. What do you mean by semantics?

Q2. How will you explain the concept 'meaning of meaning'?

Q3. Show the difference between these terms.

(i) Semantics and Pragmatics

(ii) Sentence and Utterance

(iii) Connotation and Denotation

(iv) Entailment and Presupposition

(v) Text and Discourse

(vi) Sense and Reference

(vii) Gradable and Non-gradable adjectives

Q4. What are synonyms? Give five examples of synonymy.

Q5. What are antonyms? Give five examples of it.

Q6. What are homonyms? Give its five examples.

Q7. How is homonym different from homograph? Give examples to make it clear.

Q8. What is polysemy? Give its examples.

Q9. What is hyponymy? Give its examples.

Q10. What is referential theory of meaning? Elucidate it with some examples.

Q11. What is contextual theory of meaning? Write down its features with some examples.

Q12. What is componential theory of analysis? Mention its characteristics.

Q13. What do you mean by Transformational Generative theory of meaning? Mention its features with examples.

Q14. Write down the meaning of the following words according to the componential analysis theory.

(i) Horse (ii) Camel (iii) Child
(iv) Mare (v) Woman (vi) Tree

Q15. Write down the antonyms and synonyms of the following words.

(i) Happiness (ii) Intelligent
(iii) Laborious (iv) Rich
(v) Beautiful (vi) Right
(vii) Cruel (viii) Simple
(ix) Honest (x) Costly
(xi) Generous (xii) Narrow

Q16. Write down hyponyms of the following words.

(i) Black (ii) Rice (iii) Orange
(iv) Dog (v) Shirt (vi) Pea-cock

Writing System (Graphology)

11

11.1 The Significance of Writing System

It is an undeniable fact that language came into existence in spoken form and writing system emerged as a later development. A sensible glance at the history of civilization reveals that mankind has developed different kinds of art forms or systems in order to suffice all those needs, which were realised to be very significant in making human life better. The development of writing system can better be understood from this perspective. With the advancement of society, our communicative requirements also grew faster and we began to realise the need of a more comprehensive form of language. The spoken form of language fell short of fulfilling the communicative requirements because of the widening horizon of human interaction and it led to the development of written form of language.

Writing as a constituent of language serves many communicative purposes, which cannot be done by speech. The functions exclusively performed by writing can be enumerated as follows.

(a) It helps us in preservation of knowledge coming down the ages, as a vast amount of information cannot be stored in our memory for a long time. We come to know about our ancient achievements in every walk of life through written records.

(b) It works as an authentic document for any kind of deal or treaty that involves two or more than two parties. Any written document is very reliable in the sense that it cannot be easily tampered with.

(c) It is useful in passing on instructions or suggestions to a large number of people for the sake of smooth administration. The scope of misinterpretation can be considerably minimised in written materials. Through writings, a uniform appeal may be made to a large number of people, which is often needed particularly within the boundary of a nation.

(d) It is the most powerful source of dissemination of knowledge and information that transcends the limit of time and space, i.e. one can read the sources of information as per one's own convenience. The spread of education through books is its good example.

(e) The state of development of any language can largely be measured in terms of writings available in it. We can estimate the number of words used in a language or its literary productions through writings only.

The importance of writing can be evidenced further by the fact that the pace of advancement of modern civilization increased manifold after the invention of printing press. It would not be an overemphasis to say that it is writing as a component of language that chiefly contributed to the expansion of knowledge all around the world that finally set the modern, technologically advanced society on a very strong pedestal. Thus, writing has played a very significant role in enriching modern civilization from all the possible angles. The emergence of writing added many new attributes to language as an indispensable entity.

11.2 A Brief History of Writing

In order to understand the writing system comprehensively, it's important to survey its whole journey from the point of origin to the modern state. For this sake, let us divide the writing system into two parts.

11.2.1 Ancient Writing System

An attempt to explore the root of writing leads us to a conclusion that the inspiration for developing writing came from drawings, one of the artistic attributes of mankind. History has recorded some drawings or carvings, which date back to more than 10000 years. As we know that the main idea behind any drawing is usually to transfer an impression, this worked as the source of inspiration that resulted into emergence of writing in later phases. In the beginning, the pictures of things were drawn to communicate in absence. Further, the pictures of sun, tree, fish, cloud, etc. were drawn to represent such things in non-verbal contexts. This representation through pictures is technically called pictograms. Later on, certain ideas related to some objects were expressed through the pictures, such as light through the sun , while shade through the tree , etc. This indicated a shift in the direction of expression of some abstractions related to some concrete objects. This is technically called ideogram. The journey from pictogram to ideogram was a remarkable step in the direction of evolution of writing-system. We came across the uses of pictograms and ideograms in ancient civilizations like Sumerian, Egyptian, Indus valley, etc.

On the basis of the records available today, it has been established that the people of Sumerian civilization (mid-west Asia) started inscribing on clay during 3100 BC for the sake of non-verbal communication and other administrative works. These people were engaged in trade that necessitated maintaining record, accounts, etc. Their style of inscription is called cuneiform (wedge-shaped) as the symbols used, appear like wedges. This was clearly an improvement upon pictogram and ideogram. Here the wedge like symbols were used to represent the ideas associated with many things with the change in number and position of such symbols. This cuneiform representation became very important in the sense that it led to almost complete transformation of pictorial or ideographic forms. The way of expression of objects in terms of certain symbols paved the way for the concept of word. Therefore, cuneiform style is called logogram on the line of pictogram and ideogram, as it presented the symbols that may be treated to be parallel to words of later phases.

Pictogram	**Ideogram**	**logogram**
		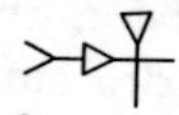
Sun	Heat, God	Star
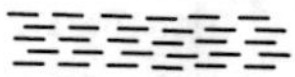	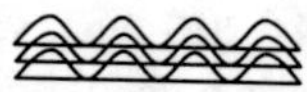	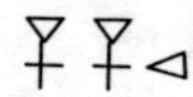
Water	Current, Thirst	Fish

The symbols used above clearly indicate that in logogram a remarkable shift took place where the picture of the objects became largely insignificant, as a set of symbols (wedges) replaced the picture. It led to the emergence of word writing system with passage of time. In addition to these forms of writings, a different form known as 'rebus' was also in use. In this form, symbols and pictures were put together as the part of a word or sentence to convey the idea.

For example,

My	son	is an	eye opener
M 		is an	 opener (Rebus)
I	believe in		moonworship
	believe in		 worship (Rebus)

We find that the picture of eye  is used as part of a word or as an independent word also, in this form of writing. It indicates the relationship between a symbol and the sound produced to represent it. When this sound is used as a part of a word or sentence, its corresponding symbol is used, without taking into account its meaning feature. It is to some extent, similar to the present use of language in electronic mails and sms where we write sentences like—ICU for 'I see you' an example of sound-symbol correspondence. It is assumed that this concept of making a word with different kinds of constituents led to the development of syllabic form of writing.

The writing system followed by Egyptians a parallel civilization to Sumerians, was a mixture of pictogram and ideogram that was named 'hieroglyphics' (sacred carvings) by the Greeks later on, as they had trade relations with these people. On the basis of records available and facts mentioned above, it can be said with certainty that the writing system has started its journey from the pictogram and it has resulted into various modern forms of writing with the passage of time.

11.2.2 Modern Writings

Any modern writing system is a product of gradual modification in its pre-existing forms. These modifications have occurred due to the several factors such as inter-cultural contacts, trade relations, scientific advancements of human societies in general, etc. A close look at all the modern forms of writings leads us to the point that these forms can be divided into three categories—morphemic, syllabic and alphabetic depending on the style followed. Let us talk about these one by one.

11.2.2.1 Morphemic writing

It is that form of writing in which one graphic sign represents one word (a morpheme). This sign used, indicates the meaning of the word also. The old pictorial form of writing still predominantly followed in Chinese language is an example of morphemic writing. Any object or the abstraction which may be associated with this object is represented pictorially in this kind of writing. Because of this nature of morphemic writing system, there are thousands of graphic signs that need to be kept in mind by the users of such languages for successful communication. In this writing system, the pronunciation of a word itself gives the meaning of the word unlike English where you cannot know the meaning of a word even after knowing the way it is pronounced. Morphemic writing system shows a logical connection between the object or the abstraction intended to be expressed, and the graphic sign used to represent it. For example, the graphic sign for a mountain will be big, and for an ant, small in such languages. In addition to it, the graphic signs for a mountain and an ant will largely be the miniature picture of these two, in order to maintain one sign one meaning correspondence. Thus, we find in the symbol itself a phonetic-semantic link as pronunciation leads to meaning in this writing system.

11.2.2.2 Syllabic writing

As the name implies, here the syllables of a language are represented by the symbols in writing. In this writing, one syllable-one symbol correspondence is observed. This feature is found predominantly in Japanese and Cherokee languages. The phonetic realization of a syllable is represented by one symbol in these languages which can be illustrated like this.

Japanese	Cherokee
< ま > "ma"	< Ꭹ > "gu"
< ほ >"ho"	<Ꭷ > "ka"
< た >"ta"	<Ꮤ > "ta"

These syllables clearly indicate that they are combinations of consonant and vowel sounds that constitute words. On the basis of these examples, we can understand the difference in writing system of English (alphabetic) and these two languages. In English, we have separate symbols for consonant and vowel constituents of a syllable unlike these two languages where one symbol represents both consonant and vowel sounds. This form of writing is suitable for those languages in which consonant clusters are not found.

11.2.2.3 Alphabetic writing

In this writing system, each sound is represented by a separate symbol. That is to say, the word 'cat' of English has got three sounds /k/, /æ/ and /t/, and each one is represented by the symbols (alphabet) 'c', 'a' and 't' respectively. Therefore, English has an alphabetic system along with the majority of the European languages. This system of writing was popularized by the Greek civilization. The people of Greek had trade relations with Phoenicians (Sumerians and Egyptians). The Greek adopted many of their symbols based on similarity in pronunciation. In the language of Phoenicians (ancient Arabic), vowel sounds were not represented through separate symbols in writing. The Greek adopted for their vowel sounds all those symbols used by Phoenicians which were in addition to the similar consonant sounds between the two languages. This was the first step in the development of alphabetic system for which the Greek should be credited. Later on, it was passed on to Romans who spread it in many societies.

The alphabetic writing system suits the scientific nature of mankind as it appears to be logical in representation of both consonant and vowel sounds. Further, it is being accepted in many other writing systems because it is suitable for transcription. Because of these factors only, the alphabetic form of writing has crept into Chinese and Japanese languages as well where it seems challenging to transcribe the foreign words with traditional writing forms—morphemic and syllabic.

The alphabetic system includes those languages also where vowel sounds are not represented through separate alphabetic symbols in all the cases. For instance, in Arabic language, separate alphabet is not there for vowels. The vowel sounds are represented through certain signs which are used with consonantal alphabetic symbols. In Hindi, separate alphabet is there for consonants and vowels, but in majority of the cases, vowels are represented through certain signs which are used with consonantal alphabetic symbols. This phenomenon practised in these languages gives an impression that they are close to syllabic form of language. But the basic difference between these languages and syllabic languages is that in these languages each vowel sound is represented by a separate sign, and therefore, a logical connection exists between the vowel sound and its sign.

Hindi	Arabic	Cherokee
गा "ga"	كي "ki:"	J "gu"
दा "da"	مي "mi:"	Γ "hu"

These examples clearly indicate that in Hindi and Arabic, the signs used for vowel sounds are uniform, that is, they represent the same sound regardless of the consonantal alphabet. This is not the case with Cherokee language (Syllabic form) where the vowel sound "u" does not have a separate sign of uniform nature. On this basis, it is quite logical to say that Arabic and Hindi follow alphabetic system not syllabic system.

11.3 Some Concepts in Writing System

In order to make a scientific study of writing system, certain specific terms are used here also as we have done in phonology or morphology, etc. Let us talk about these terms.

11.3.1 Grapheme

A grapheme is that minimal distinct symbol in the writing system of a language which represents a morpheme in the morphemic system, a syllable in the syllabic system and an alphabet in the alphabetic system of writing. For instance, we have seen in the morphemic system of writing that the symbols like < & >, < 2 >, < = >, etc. represent complete meaning and so, such symbols are the graphemes in this kind of writing system. Likewise, a symbol < Ꮷ > that represents one syllable in Cherokee language is a grapheme of this language and an alphabet like < k > is a grapheme of English language. Thus a grapheme is that concept associated with writing system (graphology) which expresses the similar kind of relationship that exists between phoneme and phonology, morpheme and morphology. Depending on the nature of writing system, a grapheme can be divided into three types—morphemic, syllabic and alphabetic. A grapheme is usually shown in angular brackets < >.

11.3.2 Allograph

The variants of graphemes are called allograph. A grapheme may be represented in more than one form, and so, these alternative realizations are allographs. For example, 'B' and 'b' are the allographs of the grapheme < b >. These allographs stand with graphemes in the same kind of relationship that is found between phonemes and allophones.

11.3.3 Digraph

When two graphemes are used to represent one phoneme, they are digraphs. The first two letters of the words 'shop' 'chair', etc. are digraphs as they jointly represent the phonemes /ʃ/ and /tʃ/ respectively of the English language.

11.4 English Orthography (Spelling-Pronunciation Interface)

The orthography of English has its roots in Latin alphabet. The Roman missionaries came to England in 7th century to propagate Christianity and under their influence, an almost complete shift took place in the writing system from runic alphabet (used by the then Germanic invaders) to modern English alphabet. Because of the several distinctive factors such as political, racial, regional, religious, etc., a lack of uniformity was found in the spelling of words used by different social groups in England. Moreover, society was not well-developed to maintain the uniformity of spellings even it was not realised as something important. The use of language was largely confined to speech only. With the advancement in age, England went on occupying a central stage in international arena that caused heavy borrowings of words from different sources. The growth of literature coupled with the political stability started paving the way for uniformity of spellings.

The Renaissance and the invention of printing press brought about a massive revolution, especially in the academic world. It led to the growth of wider interest among people towards acquiring new knowledge. It was largely realized that spellings of majority of the words did not represent the sounds used in their pronunciation. The major factor responsible for this difference was the diversity of the sources of words and their users, i.e. the distinctive phonological features of each speech community affected the pronunciation of the loan words in different ways. This phenomenon significantly increased the lack of correspondence between spelling and pronunciation. Apart from this, in the early phase of invention of the printing press, most of the people involved in printing work were Dutch who did not have good idea of pronunciation of English words. Further, they had no concern for stabilization or fixation of the spellings. Not only that, even they used to delete or add the letter 'e' at last of a word if it helped them to adjust the margins neatly. Therefore, the advent of the printing press also could not bring about the expected uniformity in spellings as the words were printed in the way the writers had spelt. The situation was so chaotic that the same writer used to write the same word with different spelling. These variations were widely observed in vowels. The letters 'iI' 'ee' 'y' 'etc', were interchangeably used. For instance, the word 'been' is found as 'bin' 'been' and 'beene'; 'fellow' as 'felow' 'felowe', 'fellow', 'fallow', 'fallowe', and likewise the case with many other words. The dissemination of knowledge and reading materials brought forth by printing press generated a fresh interest among the readers who realised the need of uniformity in spellings. This lack of uniformity in spelling was immensely responsible for the lack of uniformity in pronunciation.

Another important development in this area that appeared after renaissance was the use of that spelling which may show its etymological link. This feature can be looked upon as a glorification of ancient knowledge that was revealed after renaissance. For instance, the word 'debt' was written as 'dette' in Middle English, in which 'b' letter was inserted to show its Latin source 'debitum'. The spelling of the words like receipt, doubt, indict, etc. are the results of post renaissance development. A major development in the direction of stabilizing the spelling of words took place with the compilation of a dictionary of English language by Dr. Johnson in 1755. This ongoing tradition of lexicography has undoubtedly contributed significantly to the fixation of spellings and pronunciations.

In the light of these observations, we can understand the reasons behind discrepancy between spelling and pronunciation of English words continuing till date. The emergence of England as a major force in the preceding centuries coupled with the literary enrichment brought about uniformity in spellings to a large extent in Modern English. But in the last century, American influence at the global level started making inroads in the established uniformity. Some American literary figures came out with the notion of Americanization of English language. The growth of this feeling can largely be attributed to the emergence of America as the global leader, especially in the second half of the 20th century. This wave of the Americanization of the English language championed by the people like Daniel Webster got wide support. As a result, today, we find the global acceptance of spellings like color, program, favor, labor, etc. This Americanization of the English language has significantly added to the diversity of spellings once again, causing much confusion, especially to the non-native English learners.

It is relevant to mention in this context another potential source, the use of English in information-technology, (computer-mobile) that has initiated the use of a new form of English language where '*c*' '*r*' '*u*', etc. the letters are used to represent the words "see" "are" and "you" respectively because of the similarity in the pronunciation of the letters and words. In the years to come we may come across many kinds of changes further in English.

Exercises

Q1. What is the importance of writing in any language?

Q2. Write a note on the history of writing system.

Q3. Write short notes on the following.

(a) Pictogram	(b) Ideogram
(c) Logogram	(d) Grapheme
(e) Morphemic writing	(f) Syllabic writing
(g) Allograph	(h) Digraph

Q4. What are the main causes of spelling-pronunciation discrepancy in English language?

Q5. Give a brief account of different kinds of influences on English orthography.

Answers to Some Exercises

Chapter 7. Morphology

Q8. Tree-diagrams of morphemes with labels

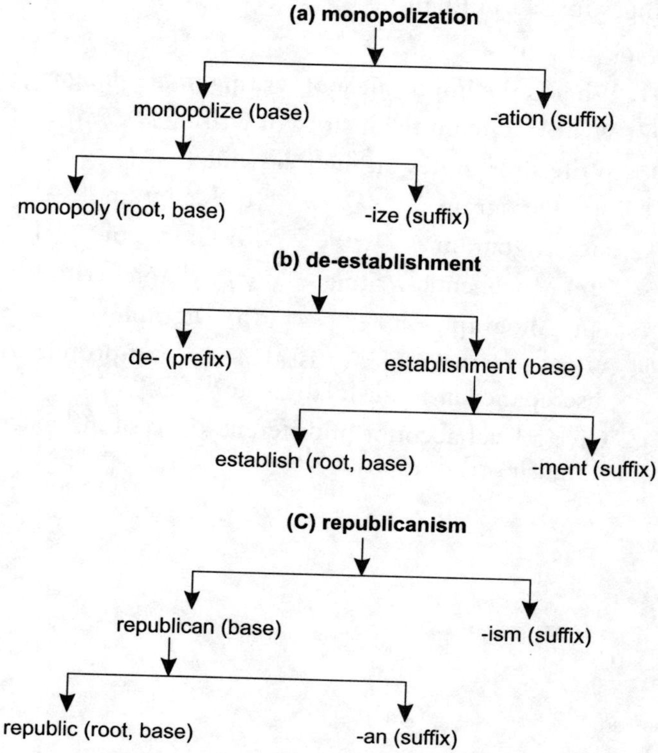

(d) unconventional

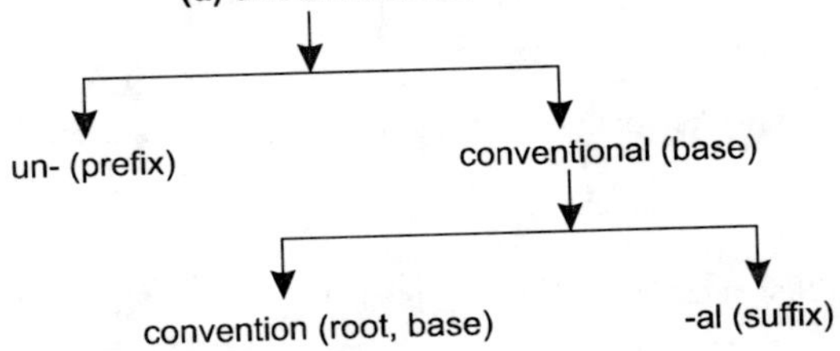

(e) neo-classicism

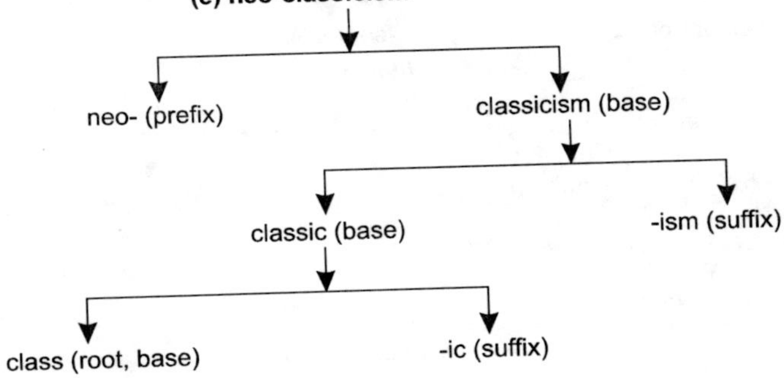

(f) reinvestment

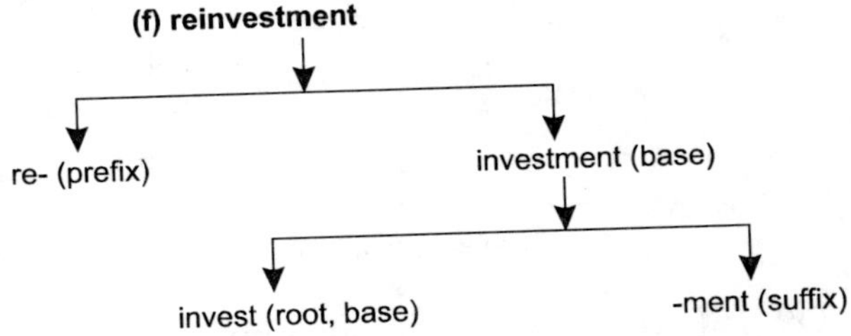

(g) pentasyllabic

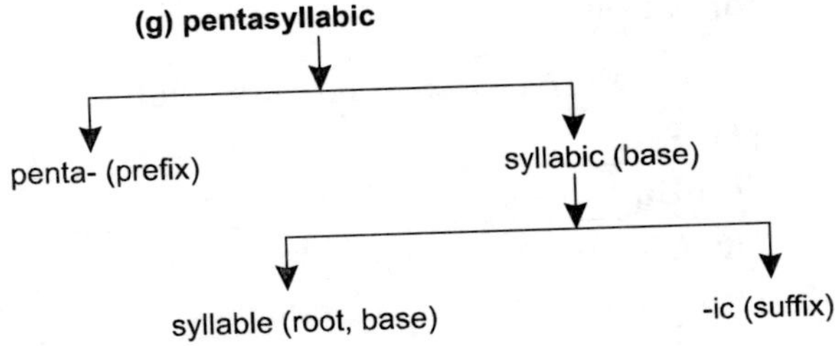

(h) marketeers'

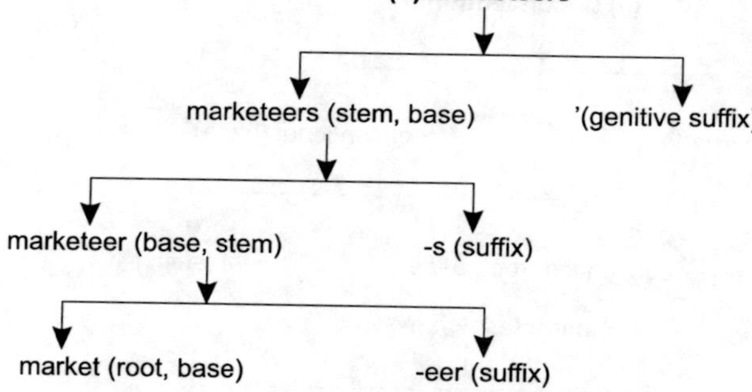

(i) horrifying

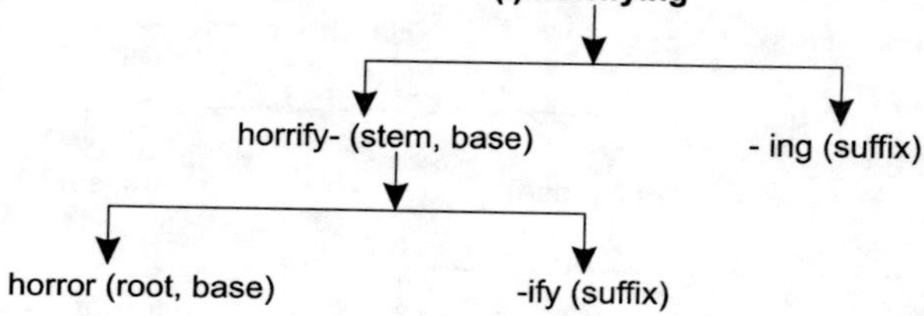

(j) immorality

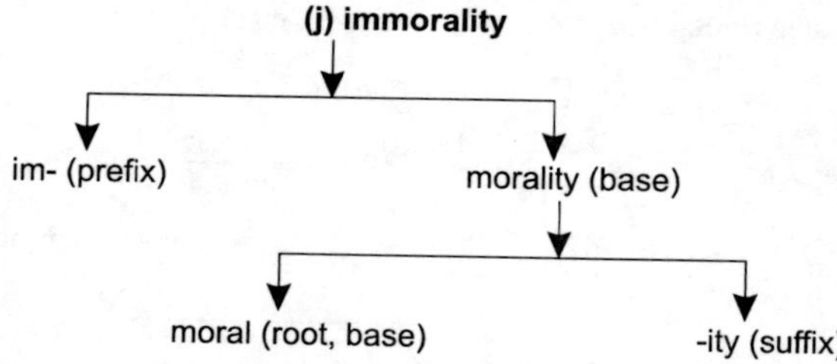

Q9. Different words and the process involved in their formation—

Words	Process involved
(a) Play	Conversion
(b) Unresolved	Derivation
(c) Classroom	Compounding
(d) Motel	Blending
(e) Oxbridge	Blending
(f) IMF	Acronymy
(g) Telecast	Blending

Words	Process involved
(h) Comfy	Multiple formation
(i) Helter-skelter	Duplication
(j) Fridge	Clipping
(k) Behave	Back formation
(l) Goldmines	Compounding
(m) Inform	Back formation
(n) Nitty-gritty	Duplication
(o) Over-burdened	Compounding

Chapter 8. Syntax

Q13. Different parts of the noun phrases—

(a) Most of (Quantifier) those (Det.) good (Adj.) singers (Noun)

(b) An (Det.) ill-built (Adj.) house (Noun) in Ranchi (Preop. Ph)

(c) The (Det.) most (Intensifier (degree)) interesting (Adj.) Greek (Classifier) plays (Noun)

(d) All (Quantifier) the (Det.) first (Ordinal) five (Cardinal) novels (Noun) of Dickens (Preop. Ph)

(e) Some of (Quantifier) the (Det.) very (Intensifier) bright (Adj.) English (Classifier) students (Noun)

(Here all the quantifiers may be considered as pre-determiners as well because they come before the determiners).

Q.14. Tree-diagrams of phrase structure

(a) Abdullah runs a shop.

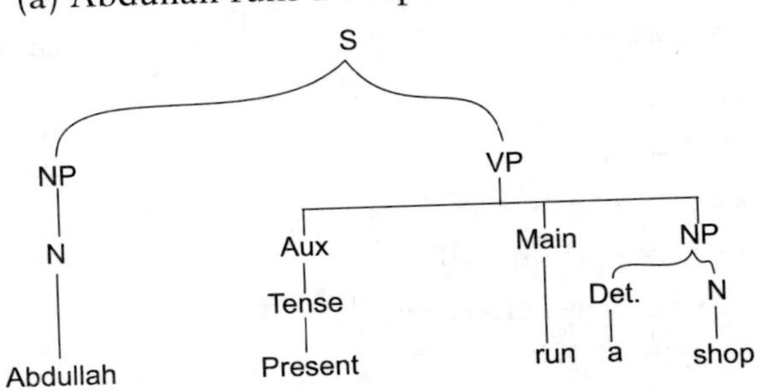

P-S rule:

S → NP – VP

NP → (Det) – N

VP → Aux – Main – NP

(b) That boy is working hard.

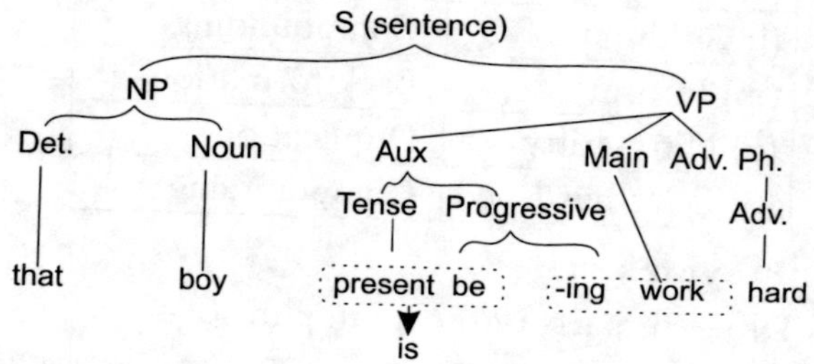

P-S rule:

S → NP – VP

NP → Det – N

VP → Aux – Main – Adv. Ph

Aux → Tense – Progressive

(c) The best students have topped in the examination.

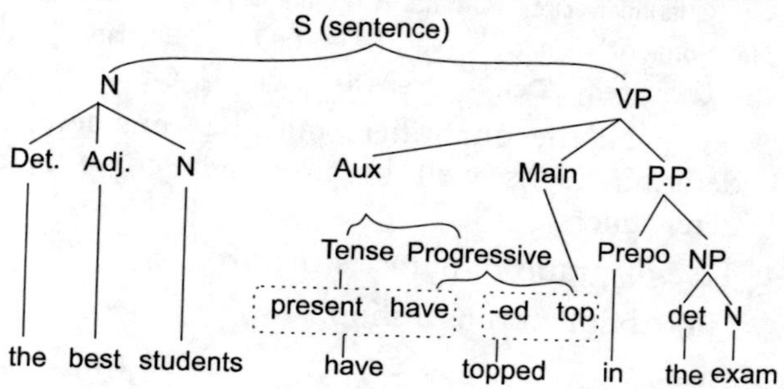

P-S rule:

S → NP – VP

NP → Det – (Adj) – N

VP → Aux – Main – PP

Aux → Tense – Perfective

PP → Prepo – NP

(d) Those students may have gone for a picnic.

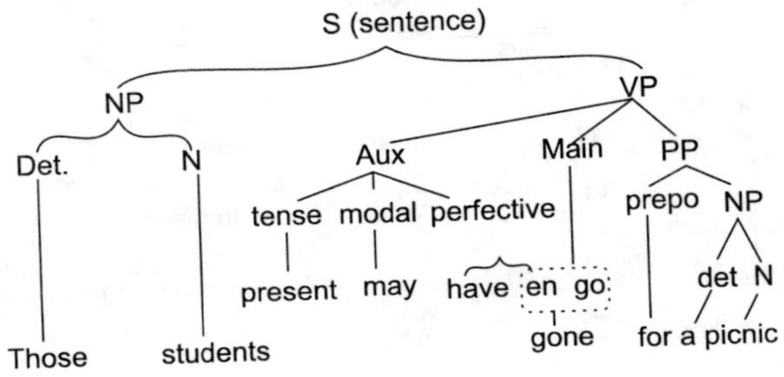

P-S rule:

S → NP – VP

NP → Det – N

VP → Aux – Main – PP

Aux → Tense – Modal – Perfective

PP → Prep – NP

(e) My friend is very short.

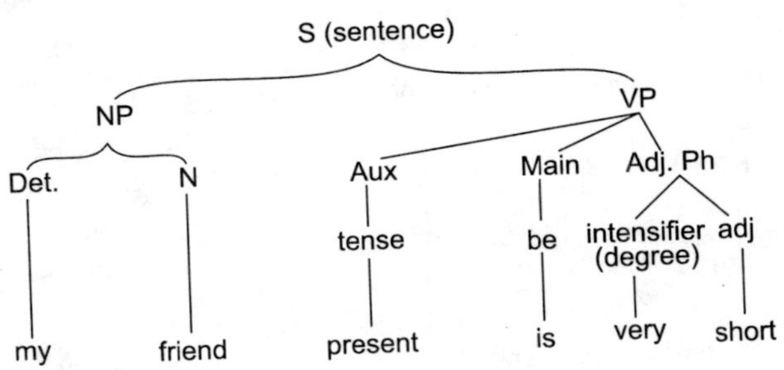

P-S rule:

S → NP – VP

NP → Det – N

VP → Aux – Main – Adj. Ph

Adj. Ph → Intensifier – Adj.

(f) The teacher said that the earth is round.

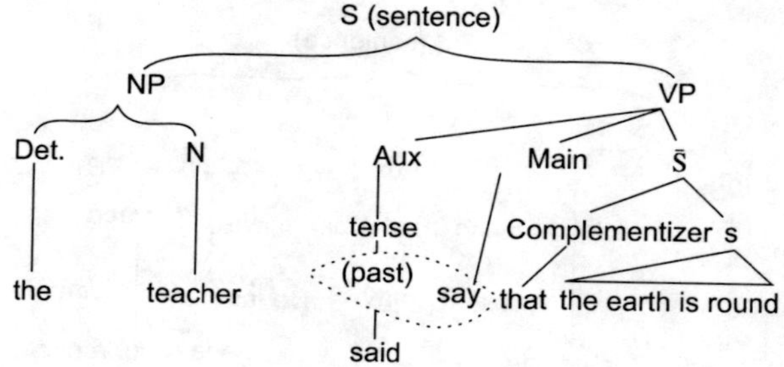

P-S rule:

S → NP – VP

NP → Det – N

VP → Aux – Main –S̄

S̄ → Complementizer – S

(g) He was playing and I was reading.

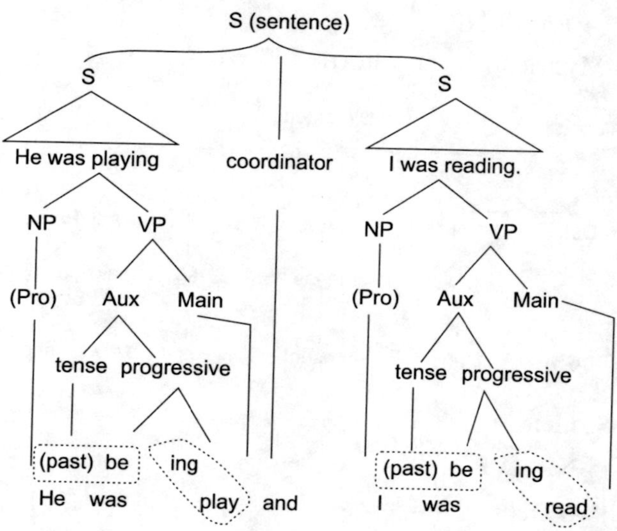

P-S rule:

S → NP – VP

NP → N (Pro)

VP → Aux – Main

Aux → Tense – Progressive

(h) I came when it was raining.

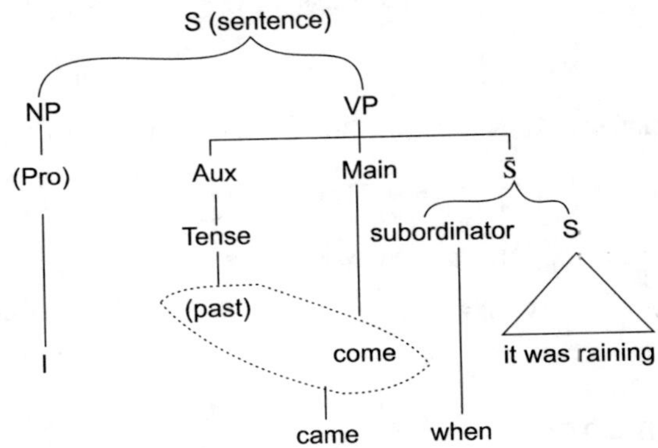

P-S rule:

S → NP – VP

NP → N(pro)

VP → Aux – Main – S̄

S̄ → Subordinator – S

(i) He may have been being rewarded.

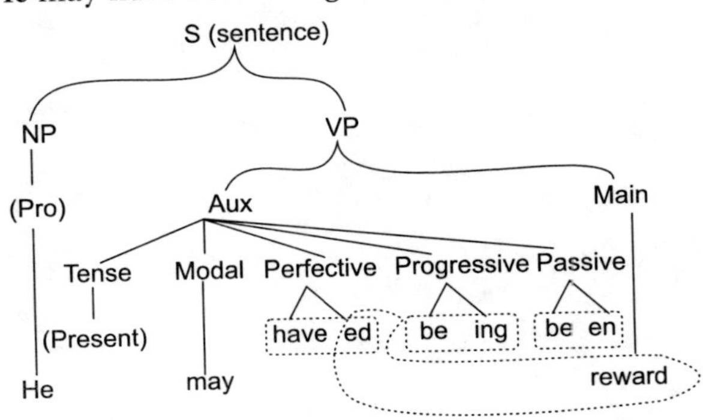

P-S rule:

S → NP – VP

NP → N(Pro)

VP → Aux – Main

Aux → Tense – Modal – Perfective – Progressive– Passive

(j) Those people will be leaving tomorrow.

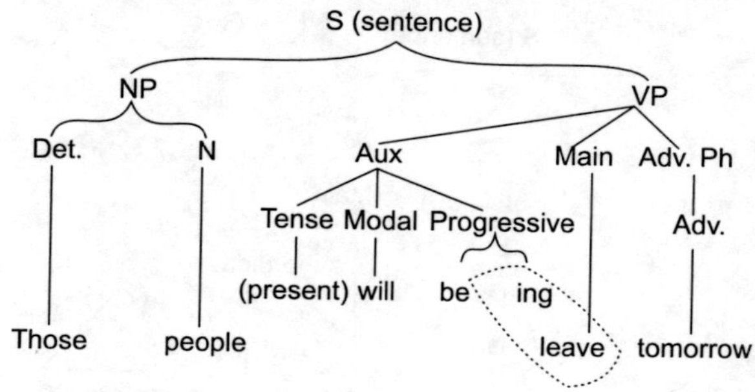

P-S rule:

S → NP – VP

NP → Det. – N

VP → Aux – Main – Adv. Ph

Aux → Tense – Modal – Progressive

Bibliography

Aarts, F. and J. Aarts (1982). *English Syntactic Structures: Functions and Categories in Sentence Analysis*, Pergamon Press: Oxford.

Adger, D. (2003). *Core Syntax: A Minimalist Approach*, Oxford University Press: Oxford.

Baker, A. (1982). *Introducing English Pronunciation*, Cambridge University Press: Cambridge.

Balasubramanian, T. (1996). *A Textbook of Phonetics*, Macmillan India Press.

Baltin, M. and C. Collins (2001). *The Handbook of Contemporary Syntactic Theory* (edited), Blackwell: Oxford.

Bauer, L. (1988). *Introducing Linguistic Morphology*, Edinburgh University Press: Edinburgh.

Black, B. (1990). *Relational Grammar*, Routledge: New York.

Blakemore, D. (1992). *Understanding Utterances*, Blackwell: Oxford.

Carter, R. and Michael McCarthy (2006). *Cambridge Grammar of English*, Cambridge University Press.

Catford, J.C. (1988). *A Practical Introduction to Phonetics*, Oxford University Press.

Chomsky, N. (1965). *Aspects of the Theory of Syntax*, MIT Press: Massachusetts.

—— (1980). *Rules and Representations*, Blackwell: Oxford.

—— (1986). *Barriers*, MIT Press: Cambridge.

—— (1995). *Minimalist Programme*, MIT Press: Cambridge.

Cook, V.J. and Mark Newson (1988). *Chomsky's Universal Grammar: An Introduction*, Blackwell Publishers: Oxford.

Cowan, R. (2008). *The Teacher's Grammar of English*, Cambridge University Press.

Cruttenden, A. (1994). *Gimson's Pronunciation of English*, 5th edition, Gimson's original book revised and edited, Edward Arnold: London.

Crystal, David (1989). *Linguistics*, Pelican Books.

—— (1988). *Cambridge Encyclopaedia of Language*, Cambridge University Press.

Formkin, V. and Robert Rodman (1993). *An Introduction to Language*, Harcourt Brace College Publishers: New York.

Giegerich, H.J. (1992). *English Phonology: An Introduction*, Cambridge University Press: Cambridge.

Griffiths, P. (2006). *An Introduction to English Semantics and Pragmatics*, Edinburgh University Press.

Harris, J. (1994). *English Sound Structure*, Blackwell: Oxford.

Heageman, L. (1991). *An Introduction to Government and Binding Theory*, Blackwell: Oxford.

Horrocks, G. (1987). *Generative Grammar*, Longman: London.

Hurford, J.R. and B. Heasley (1983). *Semantics: A Coursebook*, Cambridge University Press.

International Phonetic Association (1999). *Handbook of the International Phonetic Association*, Cambridge University Press: Cambridge.

Ladefoged, P. (2000). *Vowels and Consonants*, Blackwell: Oxford.

Leech, Geoffrey (1974). *Semantics*, Penguin Books.

Lyons, John (1992). *Language and Linguistics: An Introduction*, Cambridge University Press.

Matthews, P.H. (1974). *Morphology*, Cambridge University Press.

O'Connor, J.D. (1991). *Phonetics*, Penguin: London.

Ostler, Nicholas (2005). *Empires of the Word: A Language History of the World*, Harper-Collins: London.

Poole, S.C. (1999). *An Introduction to Linguistics*, Macmillan Press Ltd: London.

Quirk, Randolph and Sidney Greenbaum (1973). *A University Grammar of English*, Longman: London.

Radford, A., A. Martin and B. David (1999). *Linguistics: An Introduction*, Cambridge University Press.

Radford, Andrew (1988). *Transformational Grammar: A First Course*, Cambridge University Press.

Radford, Andrew (1997). *Syntax: A Minimalist Introduction*, Cambridge University Press.

Roach, P. (1983). *English Phonetics and Phonology*, Cambridge University Press.

Sinha, R.P. (2002). *Current English Grammar and Usage*, Oxford University Press: Delhi.

Spencer, A.J. (1991). *Morphological Theory*, Blackwell: Oxford.

Tallerman, M. (1998). *Understanding Syntax*, Edward Arnold: London.

Thomas, L. (1993). *Beginning Syntax*, Blackwell Publishers: Oxford.

Verma, S.K. and N. Krishnaswamy (1989). *Modern Linguistics*, Oxford University Press: Delhi.

Williams, E. (1994). *Thematic Structures in Syntax*, MIT Press: Cambridge.

Yule, George (1996). *Pragmatics*, Oxford University Press.

—— (1985). *The Study of Language: An Introduction*, Cambridge University Press.

Index

A

ablaut, 32
Acoustic, 46
Affricates, 65-66
allograph, 190
Allomorphs, 91
amplitude, 46
aphasia, 144
Apollonius, 30
Approximants, 65, 68
Aquinas, St. Thomas, 31
Arabic, 189
arbitrariness, 5
arguments, 149, 155-57
Aspiration, 77, 87
Astadhayayi, 29
audiometer, 14
Auditory, 47

B

Back-formation, 109
Base, 102
behaviourist, 33
Blending, 110, 196
Bloomfield, 24, 29, 33, 36, 126

C

Cardinal, 58, 116, 197
cascade, 144
Cherokee, 188-90
Chimpsky, 8
Chomsky, Noam, 2, 22, 34, 36, 40, 131, 142
Clipping, 109, 197
cognitive, 23, 34, 144
Coherence, 169
Columbus, 31
competence, 34, 40, 145, 150
Componential Analysis, 177
computational system, 149, 161-63
connotative, 23, 166, 171
Cratylus, 30
cryptography, 27
cuneiform, 185

D

Denotative, 171
Determiners, 116, 153
diachrony, 33, 37
diacritics, 60
dialectal, 21

digraphs, 190
Dionysius, 30
diphthong, 59, 72-74
Discourse, 169, 181
discourse analysis, 16, 19, 25
Dobzhansky, 144
Donatus, 30-31
Dr. Johnson, 192
Dutch, 191
dyslexia, 144

E

Edward Sapir, 33
Egyptians, 186, 188
Embedding, 146
Entailment, 172, 181
Epiglottis, 50
ethnolinguistics, 19, 25, 35

F

frequency, 46
Firth, 178
Fricatives, 65, 67

G

genotype, 144
Germanic, 191
gesture, 3, 84
Gimson, A.C., 69
grapheme, 190
graphology, 17-18, 190
Greek, 3, 29-31, 35, 140, 189, 197

H

Herris, Zelling, 34
Headedness, 146
hierarchical, 128, 152, 154-55
Hindi, 189
Holder, 32
Homonyms, 174
Hyponyms, 175

I

ideogram, 185-86
illocutionary force, 168
inflections, 29-30, 95
ingressive, 48, 52, 61
Intermittent closure, 54
interpretive, 181
intonation, 80

J

Japanese, 145, 188-89
Jones, William, 32
Juncture, 84, 86-87

K

kernel, 132-34

L

Language Acquisition Device, 143
langue, 33, 39-40
larynx, 47, 49
Laterals, 65
Lexeme, 91
Locality, 147
logical form, 162
logogram, 185-86

M

macro-linguistics, 19
Mahabhashya, 30
mental lexicon, 162
metaphysical, 164
micro-linguistics, 19-20
minimalism, 161-63
Morph, 90

morphophonemic, 91
Multiple formation, 110, 197

N

neurolinguistics, 19, 22, 145
non-discrete, 7-8
non-instinctive, 5

O

Ogden and Richards, 176
Onomatopoeia, 110
Open approximation, 54
ordinal, 116
orthographic, 43, 90, 107
Orthography, 191
oscillograph, 14

P

Panini, 29
paradigmatic, 33, 41-42
parameters, 24, 30, 52, 54, 143, 145, 148-52, 155, 162-63, 178
parole, 33, 39-40
Patanjali, 30
performance, 34, 40, 167
performative meanings, 168
permutation, 132
pharynx, 47, 50
phenotypic, 145
Phoenicians, 188
Phonemic Analysis, 77
Phonotactics, 76, 87
pictograms, 185
pitch, 46
Plato, 29-30
Plosives, 65-66
Post-modifier, 116
Potagorus, 30
Pragmatics, 18, 167-68, 181
Pre-determiner, 116
predicates, 155-56
Prefixation, 92
Presupposition, 172
Pre-modifier, 116
principles, 77, 79, 143, 145, 148-52, 155, 158, 160-63
Priscian, 30-31
Pro-drop Parameter, 148
Projection, 146
proposition, 168
Prosodic, 80
psycholinguistics, 14, 19, 22-23, 35
pulmonic egressive, 47, 54-55, 61

R

Reference, 170-71, 176, 181
Renaissance, 31, 35, 191
rhythm, 80
Robins, R.H., 2, 12
Romans, 189
Root, 102

S

Saussure, 24, 33, 35, 37-39, 41
Semantics, 167
Signified, 44-45
Signifier, 44, 45
Specific Language Impairment, 144
specifier, 152
speech act, 48, 84, 167-68
Stem, 102
stimulus-response, 181
stratification, 20
stress, 63, 80
stricture, 52, 54-55, 64, 66-68

Suffixation, 92
Sumerian civilization, 185
Synchrony, 37, 45
Syntagmatic, 41, 45

T

taxonomic artifacts, 149
TG grammar, 131, 139
Theta (Θ) Theory, 155
Thrax, 30
Triphthongs, 59

U

umlaut, 32
Universal Grammar, 23, 142, 145, 163
Utterance, 168

V

velum, 49, 51-53, 55, 66-67
Viki, 8

W

Washoe, 8
Webster, Daniel, 193

X

X-bar Theory, 151
Xhosa, 48

Z

Zulu, 48